D1003782

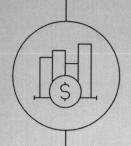

$26,240

That's how much a $10,000 investment in the SPY ETF made on October 10, 2013, would be worth as of October 10, 2023.

Investopedia
The 10 Rules of Investing

Navigating the
High-Stakes World of
Hedge Funds p. 72

How Strategy
Can Change Your
Portfolio
p. 78

Investopedia does not provide tax, investment, or financial services and advice. The information is presented without consideration of the investment objectives, risk tolerance, or financial circumstances of any specific investor and might not be suitable for all investors. Investing involves risk, including the possible loss of principal. Investors should consider engaging a financial professional to determine a suitable retirement savings and investment strategy.

1

For the Educated Investor

There are millions of articles, books, and podcasts dedicated to investing and how to do it successfully. Our own website was founded nearly a quarter of a century ago for this very reason: To provide investing and financial education to help you make smarter decisions about your money. It's still our mission today. We believe that investing is one of the best paths to building wealth and affording the life you want to live, whoever you are.

Just like playing sports, learning an instrument, or getting better at your craft or profession, when it comes to investing, fundamentals are key. Diversification, investing age-appropriately, and being tax-smart are useful in every market and through all economic cycles. Even when circumstances have changed, the fundamentals remain.

While everyone's investing game plan will be different, applying the proper fundamentals ensures that we all build long-term strategies that give us the best opportunities for returns while also protecting us from deep losses. Bear and bull markets come and go. It's knowing how to build, adjust, and maintain your portfolio that allows you to ride market waves and grow your wealth over time.

The guidance in this book leans on the expertise and advice of some of the smartest investors and financial planners we know. They practice investing fundamentals regularly with their clients and followers, and now they're sharing them with you—the educated investor.

No matter where you are on your investing journey, you're reading this because you believe that investing intelligently is the path to building your wealth so that you can live the life you want. In these pages, you'll find the tools and expertise you need to either start investing or take your knowledge to the next level.

Welcome to *The 10 Rules of Investing*—they're just the beginning of your journey toward building and growing wealth, and we're honored to be your guide.

Happy investing!

CALEB SILVER
EDITOR IN CHIEF, INVESTOPEDIA
@calebsilver

Investopedia's 10 Rules of Investing

Whether you're new to investing or a seasoned pro, these guiding principles can help you build a solid financial foundation for your future.

1 Start Now!
P. 18

2 Economy ≠ Market
P. 20

3 Time Is Everything
P. 22

4 Aim for Balance
P. 23

5 Know What You Own (and Why You Own It)
P. 24

6 Tame Your Animal Spirits
P. 26

7 Better Safe Than Sorry
P. 27

8 Manage Your Risk
P. 28

9 Be a Tax-Efficient Investor
P. 29

10 Set It, Don't Forget It
P. 30

Before Getting Started: Evaluating Your Goals and Support System

Invest some time in yourself before creating an individualized investment plan

BY DAWN PAPANDREA

Investing is a long game with lots of wins and losses along the way. If you're just starting out, sitting down and thinking through your big-picture financial goals first can help you develop the right mindset—and set you up for better outcomes.

"One of the biggest mistakes I see people make is that they just got that first high-paying job and now investing is on the table for them, but they've never really set up the systems and the habits and the behaviors that feed a good investment strategy," says Nate Hoskin, CFP, AWMA, founder and lead advisor at Hoskin Capital in Denver. What's more, many people don't take the time to set realistic goals —or any goals at all.

Here's how to think about what's important to you, how to match your goals to your values, and how to develop the systems that will support your investment strategy.

"Investing should be customized for [the individual], and there are going to be different seasons of life where [you'll want to] invest in different [assets]," says Hannah Moore, CFP, founder of Guiding Wealth, a Texas-based financial planning firm. "What's most important is making progress toward [your particular goals]."

HOW TO SET GOALS
These recommendations will help you develop a set that is right for you:

Make Abstract Ideas Measurable
Hoskin asks new clients questions

SHORT-TERM FINANCIAL GOALS

 Saving for a new car or home down payment

 Saving for a wedding or a child on the way

 Home improvements

LONG-TERM FINANCIAL GOALS

 Retirement

 College savings for a young child

 Building wealth for your loved ones to inherit

such as "What does retirement mean to you?" and "What does financial security look like?" Once that vision is defined, the next step is to come up with a dollar figure that will support it and then break it down into achievable chunks.

Rather than telling someone to save and invest until they have collected $3 million, Hoskin might suggest that a client should start with maxing out a Roth IRA every year. In 2023, the maximum contribution for a Roth is $6,500 ($7,500 if you're 50 or older). "That's going to be $541.67 a month, [which helps] make the goal feel very bite-size and achievable," he points out.

Prioritize Your Values

"Goals should be determined by values—the way you value family, relationships, and time—and those are different for everyone," says Shane Enete, Ph.D., CFA, CFP, associate professor of finance at the Crowell School of Business at Biola University in La Mirada, Calif. "Once you align your goals to your values, you intrinsically want to do it, and then everything becomes much more motivating."

For example, someone who values travel and adventure will likely have a pretty different picture of retirement than someone who values family connections.

One might downsize their home in order to go explore the world, which would require planning for a higher cost of living in retirement.

The other might decide it's more important to them to have a larger house to accommodate children and grandchildren when they visit, which might mean making mortgage payoff a priority or adding features and upgrades to the family home to help them age in place.

Make Room for Both Short- and Long-Term Goals

"Long-term goals, particularly when you're young, are hard because they don't give you any early form of reward. Having short-term goals is a great way to create that cycle of motivation," Hoskin says.

Even though short-term goals might temporarily divert some funds away from longer-term investment goals, finding the right balance can pay benefits in the long term too. When Moore pulled back on her own retirement contributions, for instance, that short-term decision ultimately helped increase her earning potential and provided more flexibility for when she started a family, thus contributing to her long-term goals in a different way.

Be Open to Alternate Paths

Just recently, Moore decided she wanted to spend more time with her extended family, who live 1,000 miles away. But she realized there were numerous ways, with different costs, to achieve that goal: She could permanently relocate, buy a vacation home, visit periodically, or do weekly video calls. She decided on the middle-ground approach of spending part of the summer visiting.

You can do the same with your investment goals. For example, choosing a semi-retired lifestyle could free up some discretionary income to help your kids pay for college.

Understand Your Time Horizon and Risk Tolerance

Investing isn't just playing the stock market. You can also invest in bonds or other lower-volatility products, says Hoskins. "That's really what will set apart those life-milestone goals, like saving for a wedding, from the longer-term goal of retirement or financial independence," he says.

HOW TO SET A GOAL

1. Envision what your ideal end result looks like.

2. Work with a financial advisor to estimate the funds you'll need and the timeline you're working with to achieve your goal.

3. Break up the overall goal into smaller milestones.

4. Allocate and automate funds to make it easier to stick to your plan.

5. Track your progress and reassess your goals as needed.

Thinking about your timeline and how much risk you're willing to take will help you select the investments that are going to serve you the best.

FIND YOUR SUPPORT SYSTEM
Hoskins calls investment goal setting a "team sport," since other people can help keep you motivated and accountable. This includes not only your life partner and family members but also people in your professional support circle.

Personal Support Systems
Getting your household involved in investing gives everyone skin in the game. This could be anything from everyone agreeing to contribute a small, set percentage of monetary gifts toward investments or parents "matching" their kids' savings. "It can be a great learning experience for kids, and it gives the adults so many great reasons to really stick to their investing goals and be good financial examples for their family," Hoskin explains.

It's also helpful to talk to extended family and friends. "Often there can be somebody a few steps ahead of you who can give you really good advice on the next step to take in your financial wellness journey," Moore says. For example, it could be someone who just put their kid through college while yours are still in grade school.

Financial Support Systems
Myriad issues and events can interrupt your financial plans, but financial professionals can help you navigate those challenges, Enete says. "You need someone who can look at all the pieces together, because if you look at things in isolation, it can cause a lot of confusion," he says.

Start with two key people: a financial advisor and a tax accountant you can rely on, Hoskin advises. Then, as your finances become more complicated—if you amass a lot of wealth, or own multiple properties or a small business—you can enlist:
• Insurance representatives: Help with protecting your assets is important as they grow larger.
• Estate planners: Put a legal plan in place for what should happen to your assets when you pass is important for your heirs.
• Financial coaches and/or financial therapists: They can keep your money mindset on track and offer budgeting guidance and extra accountability to help focus on your goals.

And of course, "A good financial advisor can act as your quarterback and interface with all of those different people," Hoskins says.

Also important: "Find someone who's acting as what's called a fiduciary, meaning there's no commission and they're just getting paid a fee," says Enete. That way, they don't have any incentive to give you advice that's not in your best interest.

EVALUATE AND REEVALUATE
Your goals should serve as your guiding star, but revisit and tweak them regularly, and especially when you experience major life events such as marriage, divorce, having children, or buying a home.

"One of the mistakes we make is thinking financial goals are static, because they inherently do change as our life and our situation changes," says Moore.

In fact, that's been true in her own experience. Moore's retirement savings took a back seat for a while when she pulled money from her Roth IRA for a house down payment and invested in her business. Now that the business is thriving, she can focus on retirement funding. "Those decisions have been for the betterment of my family—and my finances," she says.

THE BOTTOM LINE

Investing can be very effective when your unique personal goals are the guiding force. The key is to think hard about what you want out of life and keep tabs on your investment strategy to make sure it's supporting that vision. "Investing can make reachable really big dreams that feel unreachable," Moore says. ⮌

What's Your Investing Strategy?

Ask yourself these questions to help determine what kind of investor you are and translate that to building wealth

See p. 78 to learn more about investing strategies.

There is no one-size-fits-all way to invest. However, there are some key indicators that one strategy may suit you better than another, depending on your risk tolerance, financial goals, knowledge, and time horizon. If you're new to investing or simply revisiting your strategy, this quiz may give you a place to start.

1
ASSESS YOUR RISK TOLERANCE
How comfortable are you with the possibility of losing money in pursuit of higher returns?
- **A** I am comfortable with a high level of risk in exchange for potentially higher returns.
- **B** I'm OK with some risk and have time to recoup losses if necessary.
- **C** I am risk-averse and want to protect my wealth.

2
IDENTIFY YOUR GOALS
What is your primary motivation for investing?
- **A** Building wealth fast.
- **B** Diversifying my portfolio.
- **C** Supporting my approaching retirement.

3
GAUGE YOUR EXPERTISE
At this moment, how much do you know about investing?
- **A** I feel like a seasoned pro looking for the next big opportunity.
- **B** I'm confident in what I know, but my skills are about average.
- **C** I'd consider myself a novice.

4
CONSIDER YOUR TIME HORIZON
Based on your age and financial goals, are you a short-term or long-term investor?
- **A** Long-term. Time is money.
- **B** A bit of both. I have time, but I want to play the field.
- **C** Short-term. I plan to make a big purchase or retire very soon.

5
CHECK YOUR EMOTIONS
When the economy and markets are down, how do you typically react?
- **A** I'll make quick adjustments to try and recoup lost gains.
- **B** Market volatility doesn't really faze me—I'm in it for the long haul.
- **C** Bear markets are stressful, so I keep my money as safe as possible.

Mostly A's:
AGGRESSIVE

You're seeking big gains and are willing to invest time and risk to get there. A hands-on strategy and portfolio filled with mostly stocks (80% or more) may be a good fit for you. High-yield bonds and alternative asset classes may be in the mix, too. It's also likely you have time on your side to weather market volatility.

Mostly B's:
MODERATE AND BALANCED

You're a middle-of-the-road investor looking to build wealth with little work or drama. A more moderate investing strategy, focused on 60% stocks and 40% bonds, with mutual funds and ETFs mixed in may be the sweet spot for your portfolio. You have some time to reach your goals, and you typically remain levelheaded when market changes happen.

Mostly C's:
CONSERVATIVE

You're fairly risk-averse and prioritize protecting your money. A conservative investing strategy translates to fixed-income instruments such as bonds and money market funds. Protecting your money is important to you, as you are close to retirement or still getting comfortable with market volatility.

IMPORTANT   *You can have a mix of strategies, and that's OK! It's also important to note that your financial situation and goals can change. When they do, review and adjust your investment strategy accordingly.*

Investopedia

Get Investopedia newsletters directly in your inbox each day.

How educated investors get ahead, and stay ahead, of the news that moves markets.

Pre-Market

Investopedia Daily

5 Things to Know Before Markets Open

- Meta Weighs Charging Ad-Free Subscription Fees in Europe
- Ford, General Motors Lay Off More Workers as UAW Strike Continues
- Tesla Shares Dip After Third Quarter Deliveries Miss
- Kellanova Shares Rise After Tumbling in First Day of Trading Following Kellogg Split
- Job Openings Expected to Remain Steady in JOLTS Survey

TERM OF THE DAY *from Investopedia*

Monopoly

[mə-ˈnä-p(ə-)lē]

A market structure where one seller or producer is the sole supplier of a good or service in a market.

Investopedia

Monopoly

A monopoly is a market structure where a single seller or producer assumes a dominant position in an industry or a sector. Monopolies are discouraged in free-market economies as they stifle competition and limit substitutes for consumers. In the United States, antitrust legislation is in place to restrict monopolies, ensuring that one business cannot control a market and use that control to exploit its customers.

READ MORE

SPONSORED BY INVESTOPEDIA

Trade Risk-Free With Virtual Money

SUBSCRIBE TODAY

Investing Terms You Need To Know

Learn the language essential to set yourself up for financial success

BY ANNA ATTKISSON

401(K)

A retirement savings plan with tax advantages offered by many U.S. employers. The employee who signs up for a 401(k) agrees to have a percentage of each paycheck paid into an investment account. The employer may match some or all of that contribution.

ACTIVE INVESTING

A strategy involving ongoing buying and selling activity in which assets are continuously monitored several times a day to enable an investor to exploit what are often short-term profitable conditions.

ALTERNATIVE INVESTMENT

A financial asset that does not fall into one of the conventional investment categories of equity, income, or cash. Alternative investments can include private equity or venture capital, hedge funds, managed futures, art and antiques, commodities, and derivatives contracts. Real estate is also often classified as an alternative investment.

ANNUITY

A contract between the contract holder—the annuitant—and an insurance company. In return for your contributions, the insurer promises to pay you a certain amount of money, on a periodic basis, for a specified period. Many people use these contracts as a kind of retirement-income insurance that guarantees regular income after they leave the workforce.

BEAR MARKET

A sustained period of downward-trending stock prices, often triggered by a 20% decline from near-term highs. Bear markets are often accompanied by an economic recession and high unemployment but can be opportunistic times to buy assets at depressed prices.

BOND

A fixed-income instrument that represents a loan made by an investor to a borrower (typically a corporation or government). Bond details include the end date when the principal of the loan is due to be paid to the bond owner.

BROKER

An individual or firm that acts as an intermediary between an investor and a securities exchange. The exchanges only accept orders from those who are members of that exchange, so individual traders need the services of brokers to place orders. Brokers can be paid by fees, on commission, or by the exchange directly.

BULL MARKET

A sustained period of upward trending stock prices, often triggered by a 20% increase in asset prices. Bull markets, characterized by optimism and investor confidence, tend to last for months or even years.

CAPITAL GAIN

The increase in the value of an asset relative to the price the investor originally paid for it. This can include a type of investment, such as a stock or bond, or a product purchased, such as furniture or a boat. The IRS taxes individuals on capital gains in some circumstances.

COMMODITIES

A basic good used in commerce that is interchangeable with other goods of the same kind. It often refers to a raw material, such as corn, wheat, or oil.

COMPOUND INTEREST

The interest on a loan or deposit that is calculated based on both the initial principal and the accumulated interest from previous periods. Compounding multiplies money at an accelerated rate over simple interest.

DIVERSIFICATION

A risk management strategy that mixes a wide variety of investments across various financial instruments, industries, and other categories. It aims to minimize losses by investing in areas that would react differently to the same event.

DIVIDEND

The distribution of a company's earnings to its shareholders, as determined by the company's board of directors. These are often distributed quarterly and may be paid in cash or as a reinvestment of additional stock.

DOLLAR COST AVERAGING

A strategy for both beginners and long-time investors of systematically investing equal amounts of money at regular intervals, regardless of the price of a security. This can reduce the overall impact of price volatility and lower the average cost per share in total.

EARNINGS PER SHARE (EPS)

A company's net profit divided by the number of common shares it has outstanding. The resulting number indicates how much money a company makes for each share of its stock and is a widely used metric for estimating corporate value.

EXCHANGE-TRADED FUND (ETF)

A type of pooled investment security that holds multiple underlying assets and trades on an exchange just like a stock does. An ETF can be structured to track anything from the price of an individual commodity to a large and diverse collection of securities.

EXPENSE RATIO

How much of a fund's assets are used for administrative and other operating expenses is calculated by dividing expenses by the average value of its assets under management (AUM). For investors, the resulting ratio is deducted from the fund's gross return and paid to the fund manager.

FIXED INCOME

A type of investment security that pays the investor a fixed amount of interest or dividends on a fixed schedule until its maturity date. At maturity, investors are repaid the principal amount they invested. Government and corporate bonds are the most common types of fixed-income products.

FUNDAMENTAL ANALYSIS

A method of determining a stock's real or "fair market" value. It measures a security's intrinsic value by examining related economic and financial factors. Intrinsic value is the value of an investment based on the issuing company's financial situation and current market and economic conditions.

INDEX FUND

A type of mutual fund or exchange-traded fund (ETF) with a portfolio constructed to match or track the components of a financial market index, such as the Standard & Poor's 500 Index (S&P 500). It offers broad market exposure, low operating expenses, and low portfolio turnover.

MARKET CAPITALIZATION

This refers to how much a company is worth as determined by the stock market. It is defined as the total market value of all outstanding shares, and it is calculated by multiplying the number of outstanding shares by the current market value of one share.

MUTUAL FUND

A managed fund that pools money from shareholders to invest in securities such as stocks, bonds, money market instruments, and other assets. It is operated by professional money managers who allocate the assets.

OPPORTUNITY COST

The potential benefits an individual, investor or business misses out on when choosing one alternative over another. To properly evaluate this and make informed investing decisions, the costs and benefits of each option must be considered and weighed against one another.

PASSIVE INVESTING

An investment strategy to maximize returns by minimizing buying and selling. Index investing is a common passive strategy where investors purchase a benchmark, such as the S&P 500 index, and hold it over a long time horizon.

P/E RATIO

A stock valuation metric that compares a company's current share price with its earnings per share (EPS). Investors use it to determine the relative value of a company's shares in an apples-to-apples comparison with others in the same sector.

REBALANCING

The process of returning the values of a portfolio's asset allocations, designed to match risk tolerance with desire for reward, to the levels defined by an investment plan.

RETURN ON INVESTMENT (ROI)

A popular profitability metric used to evaluate how well an investment has performed. It's designed to directly measure the amount of return on a particular investment relative to its cost, expressed as a ratio or percentage.

RISK TOLERANCE

A measure of the degree of loss an investor is willing to endure within their portfolio. Stock volatility, market swings, economic or political events, and regulatory or interest rate changes affect an investor's tolerance for risk.

ROBO ADVISOR

A digital platform that provides automated algorithmic financial planning and investment services with little to no human supervision. Typically, it asks questions about your financial situation and future goals and uses that data to offer advice and automatically invest for you.

STOCKS

Also known as equity, a stock is a security that represents the ownership of a fraction of the issuing corporation. Units of stock are called "shares," which entitle the owner to a proportion of the corporation's assets and profits equal to how much stock they own.

TAX LOSS HARVESTING

Selling securities at a loss to offset the amount of capital gains tax owed on other profitable investments. This strategy is commonly used to limit short-term capital gains.

TECHNICAL ANALYSIS

A method of analyzing and predicting stock movements based on past market data, primarily price and volume. This can be used to evaluate and identify trading opportunities.

YIELD

The earnings generated and realized on an investment over a particular period, expressed as a percentage based on the invested amount, current market value, or face value of the security.

SCAN HERE

Want to learn more financial terms?
Subscribe to the Investopedia
Term of the Day newsletter.

Youth sports cost $883 per kid per season

Which might make you ask ...
if my kid doesn't get a full ride,
can I still send them to the right school?

Everyone has financial questions. At Empower,
we're helping 18 million Americans[1] answer theirs.
Take control of your financial future at **empower.com.**

EMPOWER What's Next

ADVISE · INVEST · PLAN

Investing Playbook

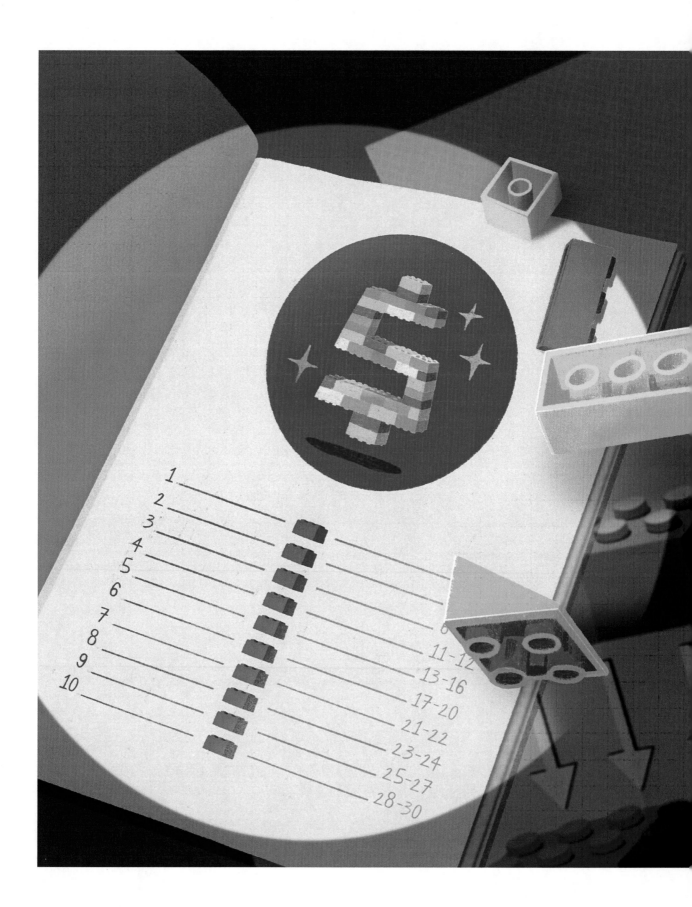

The 10 Rules of Investing

Best practices for building wealth and taking care of your future self

BY KATIE REILLY

Charlene Rhinehart, a certified public accountant who offers advice to people learning how to invest, tells all her clients to take care of their future self. "Whatever decision you make right now, make sure your future self will be happy," she says.

Rhinehart advises people to manage their expectations and recognize that investing is a long process that requires patience as well as trial and error. "Everybody looks forward to the slam dunk and making a ton of money, but you should also focus on the process," she says.

Investors should prioritize their long-term goals, including purchasing a home, paying off student debt, building a college fund, and preparing for retirement. And experts say it's important to start slowly, building your confidence and continuing to learn more about investing as you go.

Whether you're new to investing or just in need of a refresher, some key guidelines can help you navigate the process. In no particular order, here are Investopedia's 10 rules of investing.

START NOW!

The first key to investing is starting as soon as you can, putting aside money now with the goal of achieving long-term wealth, so that your future self will be in a stronger financial position. "The best time to start investing is now," Rhinehart says.

Money you invest now compounds over time, earning interest that is then reinvested, allowing the principal investment to grow. The longer you leave your money to compound, the more it will grow, generating even larger interest payments.

"You want to make sure you're taking advantage of compounding," Rhinehart says. "When you have time on your side, you have the ability to allow your investments to compound over the long term and create a more productive, prosperous portfolio."

Investing as soon as possible, and staying invested over the long run, tends to be more lucrative than waiting and trying to invest at exactly the right time, based on when the market is up or down. The latter is known as "timing the market." But because that strategy is so difficult to get right, experts say that holding onto your investments and allowing your money to spend more time in the market, is the better approach. Research by Charles Schwab concluded that "the cost of waiting for the perfect moment to invest typically exceeds the benefit of even perfect timing." Instead, the brokerage firm recommends that people invest as soon as possible, a strategy that requires less effort and expertise than timing the market.

Experts also recommend investing the same amount of money on a regular basis, thereby reducing the impact of market volatility—a practice known as dollar-cost averaging. In an ideal world, it would be best to always

How Compound Interest Grows over Time

If you invested $10,000 that compounded annually at 5%, it would be worth more than $40,000 after 30 years, having accrued more than $30,000 in compound interest.

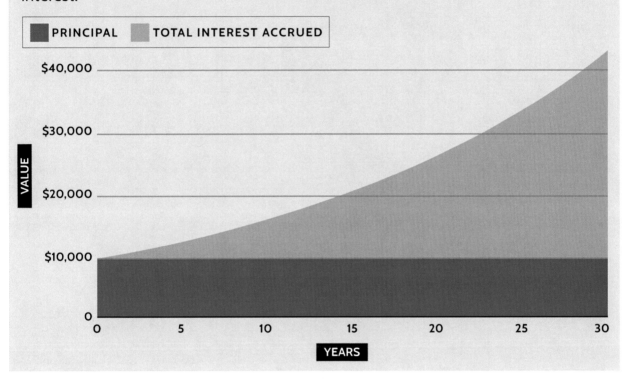

PRINCIPAL   TOTAL INTEREST ACCRUED

VALUE

$40,000

$30,000

$20,000

$10,000

0

0   5   10   15   20   25   30

YEARS

invest when the market is down and your money goes further. But timing the market is difficult even for professionals, so dollar-cost averaging is the more practical alternative. It helps investors lower their average cost per share, enabling them to take advantage of the best share prices without having to predict them in advance. This practice also helps enforce consistent investing habits.

"Stick with it and automate it," says Samantha Silberstein, a certified financial planner and wellness coach and a member of the Investopedia Financial Review Board.

Workers who put money into their employer's 401(k) retirement plan with every paycheck are engaging in dollar-cost averaging by investing a consistent amount of money regularly, regardless of the state of the market. It's a key way to build wealth over the long term.

Rhinehart often hears from people who think they don't have enough money to begin investing, but even setting aside a small amount of money each week is a good strategy. "Start where you are, and give yourself a chance to grow," she says. "If you only have $10 to invest, invest that."

"Not investing is worse than being invested during challenging markets."

–PRESTON CHERRY
Founder and President of Concurrent Financial Planning in Green Bay, Wisconsin

ECONOMY ≠ MARKET

The U.S. economy is the broad system of production, consumption, and distribution of goods and services that influences the country's wealth. A financial market is the place where people buy and sell investments, such as securities, currencies, and bonds. While the two are different, they influence each other.

When the economy is growing and business activity is expanding, that tends to lead to stock market gains, improving returns for investors. When the stock market slumps, that results in losses for investors and a decline in consumer confidence, leading people to spend less, which can cause a downturn in the economy.

"The stock market is a leading indicator of the sentiment of the country's economy. It's a reflection of how people are feeling, and money, unfortunately, is emotional," Silberstein says. "So we have to understand that there are going to be current, short-term fluctuations."

When investing, Silberstein cautions people against reacting impulsively to market changes in the short term. "Historically, the stock market has recovered from broad slumps throughout time," she says, noting that those slumps can be just minor blips in a long-term investing plan. "A three-month period over a three-year period has a very limited impact."

The goal, she says, is to continue investing for long enough that you hit some lows and enough highs, leading to slow and steady gains over time. She recommends staying invested through the highs and lows of economic cycles.

She uses 2020 as an example. In March 2020, at the start of the COVID-19 pandemic, the global economy "closed overnight," and she saw portfolio losses of 10% to 30% for

How Business-Sector Cycles Impact Market Performance

The business cycle influences the rise and fall of stock market sectors and industry groups. Certain sectors perform better than others during specific phases. Knowing where you are in the cycle can help you position your investments in the right sectors at the right time. Here, the blue corresponds to the economic world, and the green represents the stock market. The sectors of stocks at the top perform best during these phases.

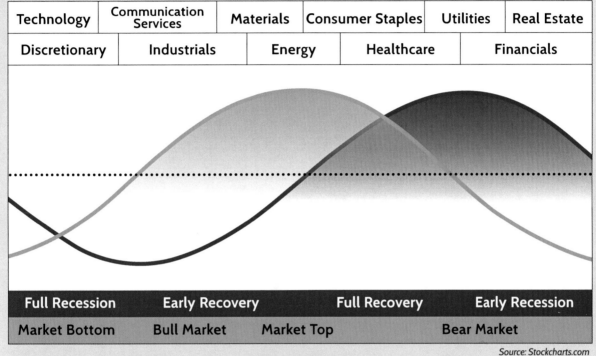

Technology	Communication Services	Materials	Consumer Staples	Utilities	Real Estate
Discretionary	Industrials	Energy	Healthcare	Financials

| Full Recession | Early Recovery | Full Recovery | Early Recession |
| Market Bottom | Bull Market | Market Top | Bear Market |

Source: Stockcharts.com

her clients that quarter. But by the end of the year, the market had improved, and Silberstein says she had clients who ended the year positively, with 20% returns in some cases.

But clients who pulled out their investments in March 2020 ended the year with a loss, she says, and many were cautious about returning to investing again.

"It's hard, emotionally and behaviorally, to get back in," says Silberstein, who witnessed similar behavior after the Great Recession in 2008. "Unfortunately, I sometimes still run across people who, after 2008, 2009, just never went back in the market. And they've missed out on the last 15-plus years of positive returns."

In 2022, the U.S. stock market experienced the biggest annual percentage decline since the 2008 financial crisis. But the market rallied in 2023. While the S&P 500 fell 19% in 2022, it had risen 14% by August 2023.

Andy Smith, a certified financial planner in Wyoming and Investopedia Financial Review Board member, says investors shouldn't let dips in the market scare them and should instead stay focused on long-term goals.

"It's going to go up and it's going to go down, and sometimes the down is going to scare the heck out of you," Smith says. "The biggest thing you cannot do is panic and take your money out. Because as history shows us, the market always comes back. And when it comes back, it usually goes to new heights."

FAST FACT

A bear market occurs when market prices decline by more than 20%, often accompanied by negative investor sentiment and declining economic prospects. Bull markets are characterized by rising prices and investor optimism.

TIME IS EVERYTHING

The right investing approach will vary for each person depending on a range of factors, including their age, stage of life, and financial goals.

While trying to time the market, discussed in our first rule, is not a sound strategy, it's important for people to consider the time in their life at which they're investing.

Those who are investing when they're young and at the beginning of their career should take a different approach than those who are older and approaching retirement. Younger investors can tolerate more risk than older investors.

"If you start younger, you have more flexibility to have more exotic assets in your portfolio, because you can recover," Rhinehart says. "But if you are nearing retirement, you want to make sure that your risk appetite matches those investments in your portfolio. You may want to reduce the stocks in your portfolio, because those are riskier than other more stable assets, like bonds."

She encourages people to think about why they're investing—to pay off student loans, to buy a house, to save for retirement—and what their time frame is.

If your goal is to buy a house, are you aiming to do that in five years or 15? If you're saving for retirement, are you aiming to retire in 20 years or 40? Investors should use those goals and timelines to determine their individual investing strategy.

Typically, young people can afford to take more risks while investing because retirement is still decades away for them.

Meanwhile, older people should pursue more stable stocks and bonds as part of a balanced portfolio.

When deciding whether to buy, sell, or hold a stock or fund, it's important to start by doing research. If a company is sustainably growing revenue year-over-year, and if the company's future earnings are predicted to grow, it could be a good time to buy that stock.

It's better to focus on details and data points that suggest long-term growth and stability rather than a short-term bump.

Investors could explore selling stocks if that company loses market share or if its earnings fall below expectations.

But experts emphasize that, especially for investors who are just starting out, it's important to play the long game, stay patient, and stick with investments over time.

"The big thing to focus on is remaining constant and steady, regardless of what's going on, as you're trying to build significant assets," Smith says. "Because trying to time the market is very difficult to do. Even the professionals don't do very well at it."

"Knowing your why will help make every other decision on your investing journey so much easier. It's so important to construct the portfolio based on those long-term goals."

–CHARLENE RHINEHART,
CPA and Investopedia Financial Review Board Member

AIM FOR BALANCE

A portfolio is the mix of all of a person's investments. A balanced portfolio includes investments in a diverse variety of assets—including stocks, bonds, mutual funds, or exchange-traded funds (ETFs)—to reduce volatility. The process of investing in those different asset classes is known as diversification.

"Don't dump all of your money into one investment," Rhinehart says. "Diversify your portfolio with different types of assets so that when one company is not performing well, all of your portfolio is not damaged because of that."

Experts recommend that investors regularly review their portfolio and make changes, or "rebalance," when necessary—maybe once a year—to make sure their portfolio is still allocated in the way they would like.

For example, if an investor built a portfolio with 60% stocks and 40%

bonds, but over time the portfolio shifted to a combination of 70% stocks and 30% bonds due to market performance, the investor could review and readjust their portfolio back to the original allocation in order to meet their financial goals.

"There is no magic mix that's going to work under every circumstance," says Gordon Scott, an Investopedia Financial Review Board member and active investor with 20 years of experience educating individual traders and investors. "But the conventional wisdom is that 60% stocks and 40% bonds is a really safe, easy way to think about it."

He suggests starting from that combination of stocks and bonds and then potentially moving smaller percentages into other investments, such as cash, gold, real estate funds, or global stocks. Scott says investing a small portion of your portfolio in global

stocks—markets in India, Singapore, or South Korea, for example—can help support balance.

"Non-U.S. markets are more volatile, so you would never want to put the majority of your money in those markets. But putting some can make sense," he says. "Having some money in there when they get into a growth cycle can really help.

"You're not going to have a situation where U.S. markets are going to increase triple digits, year after year," Scott continues. "But you could experience that in some Asian markets."

However you choose to divide your investments, it's most important to ensure that you're not investing all your money in one place. "If you were shopping at the mall and you were looking for shoes, you wouldn't buy all the same type of shoes, because they wouldn't work in all types of conditions," Rhinehart says.

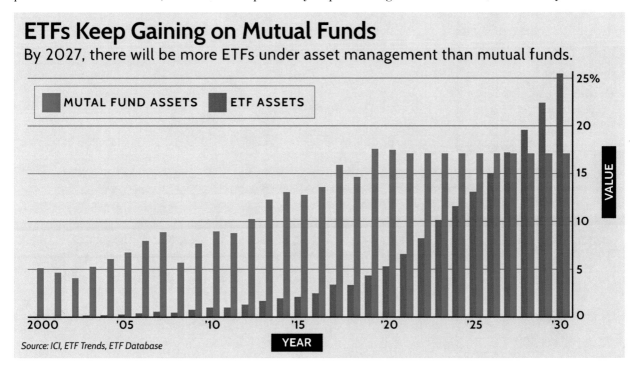

ETFs Keep Gaining on Mutual Funds
By 2027, there will be more ETFs under asset management than mutual funds.

MUTAL FUND ASSETS   **ETF ASSETS**

Source: ICI, ETF Trends, ETF Database

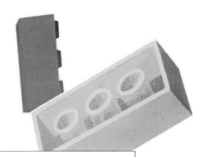

5

KNOW WHAT YOU OWN (AND WHY YOU OWN IT)

Peter Lynch, the investor famous for managing the Magellan Fund at Fidelity to great success, often advised people to "buy what you know." Smith takes that tip a step further: "Don't invest in things that you can't explain to somebody so they understand."

It's important to understand how your portfolio is allocated and what purpose each asset is serving.

When considering which stocks to buy or sell, there are several data points that are helpful to understand. Look at the market's general direction, such as the moving average of the S&P 500 Index.

If the market is trending upward overall, that likely bodes well for the individual stocks you're considering. Investors could consider pursuing a growth stock or value stock investing strategy.

Growth stocks are shares of newer companies that are expected to outperform the market over time

because they have the potential to achieve high earnings growth in the future. Value stocks are shares of a more well-established company with solid fundamentals that are priced below those of its peers at present, based on analyses of the price-to-earnings ratio, yield, and other factors.

To evaluate a bond's potential performance, consider its price compared to its face value; its maturity, which is the date when your investment will be repaid; and its yield, which is the amount the investor will receive if they hold the bond until maturity. Another useful data point is the bond's duration, which measures its sensitivity to interest rate change. A longer duration means the value of the bond will fall more as interest rates rise. A shorter duration means the value of the bond will fluctuate less.

When interest rates go up, bond prices go down, and vice versa. So

when it seems like interest rates have reached a peak and are starting to come down again, that's a good time to invest in bonds, Scott says.

Knowing what you're invested in is also critical if you're interested in putting your money toward certain issues or causes, such as environmental or social issues.

Vikram Gandhi, a senior lecturer at Harvard Business School who teaches a course on sustainable investing, recommends that investors seek out financial gains while also paying attention to the mission and actions of the companies in which they invest. Look at what they produce, what they stand for, and whether they're creating positive change in the world.

"I think there's an opportunity for even a retail investor to be investing in things that are important to them from a values [perspective]," he says, "and at the same time generating a proper return."

How To Research Stocks

Knowing what you own can start with understanding how to read a stock chart. Here are a few things worth noting when you research a stock such as Apple (AAPL), currently the largest stock by weight in the S&P 500.

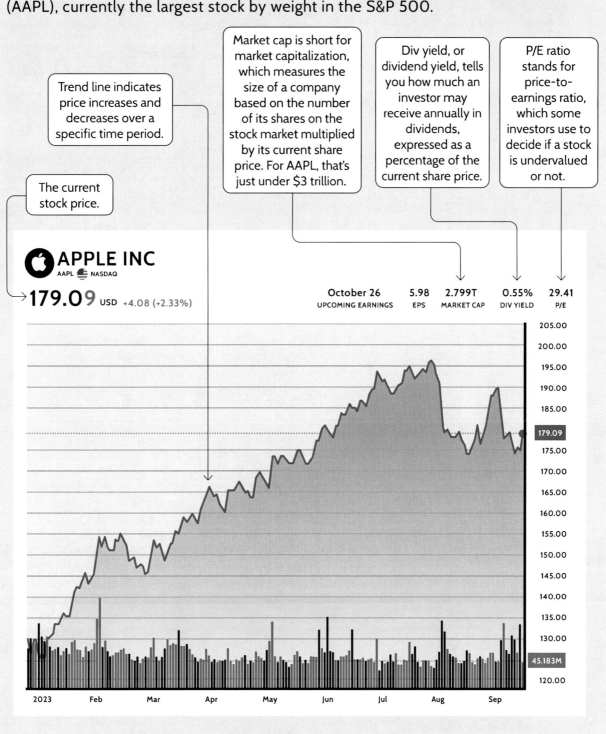

Trend line indicates price increases and decreases over a specific time period.

Market cap is short for market capitalization, which measures the size of a company based on the number of its shares on the stock market multiplied by its current share price. For AAPL, that's just under $3 trillion.

Div yield, or dividend yield, tells you how much an investor may receive annually in dividends, expressed as a percentage of the current share price.

P/E ratio stands for price-to-earnings ratio, which some investors use to decide if a stock is undervalued or not.

The current stock price.

APPLE INC
AAPL NASDAQ

179.09 USD +4.08 (+2.33%)

October 26	5.98	2.799T	0.55%	29.41
UPCOMING EARNINGS	EPS	MARKET CAP	DIV YIELD	P/E

179.09

45.183M

2023 Feb Mar Apr May Jun Jul Aug Sep

6

TAME YOUR ANIMAL SPIRITS

In 1936, John Maynard Keynes famously wrote about the animal spirits that tend to override rational decision-making when it comes to economics. People don't always act in their best interest, including when they're investing.

"If you're really fearful, it tends to make you be excessively conservative and not take risks that are good bets for the long run," says Hersh Shefrin, a professor at Santa Clara University's Leavey School of Business and an expert in behavioral finance.

On the other end of the spectrum, greed can lead people to want more than their fair share. Neither excessive fear nor excessive greed is good.

Shefrin argues that it's difficult to avoid emotions completely; they're part of being human. But finding a balance between emotion and logic is key. "We think emotionally. We think intellectually," he says. "You want those two to work together and be in balance. It's when they're unbalanced that there's a problem."

There are strategies people can use to balance their emotions and make optimal decisions. Before deciding to sell stocks, for example, experts suggest sleeping on it and reevaluating the decision in a day or two. Investors should also avoid checking their portfolios too frequently. Instead, make a plan to check in quarterly or meet with a financial advisor semi-annually. Investors should also avoid making decisions based solely on intuition.

"The thing about investing, especially for the long term, is it's a statistical game," Shefrin says. "It's misunderstanding the statistical nature of the game that leaves investors vulnerable."

Some common psychological traps include the sunk-cost fallacy, in which a person is reluctant to abandon a plan because of the resources they've already invested in it. If someone is losing money on an investment, for example, they might be tempted to stick to their strategy because of how much money they've already lost, even though it would be better to get out of that situation and take a new approach. Investors can also fall victim to confirmation bias by seeking information that reinforces their opinions, while ignoring contradicting information.

In his book *The Psychology of Investing*, John Nofsinger identified how cognitive errors, emotions and psychological biases cause people to make poor investment decisions. For example, overconfidence causes people to trade too much, resulting in lower returns. Pride causes people to sell winning stocks too soon and hold on to losing stocks too long. People tend to downplay memories of previous losses, softening their regret and leading to risky decision-making in the future.

"Unfortunately, these psychology-induced decisions create outcomes that often have negative impacts on wealth," Nofsinger wrote.

"People set goals that are too high, and they take on imprudent risks as a result—risks that, on average, don't pay off."

—HERSH SHEFRIN
Professor of finance at Santa Clara University's Leavey School of Business

BETTER SAFE THAN SORRY

Exercise caution when making big investment decisions. Do research and consider your options carefully before making any rash decisions with your money.

Smith says it's "dangerous" to borrow money to invest, noting that positive returns are not guaranteed, and investing borrowed money exacerbates the potential for negative consequences if an investment doesn't perform well. "What if what you invest in doesn't pan out?" Smith says. "You're adding unnecessary risk and taking a big chance with what losses could do to you."

Similarly, investors should think twice before tapping their retirement accounts early—in part because they will be subject to penalties if they do so, though there are some exceptions. Money withdrawn from an individual retirement account (IRA) or 401(k) plan before age 59½ is typically considered taxable income and is subject to an additional 10% tax penalty.

Taking out money prematurely also interrupts the tax-deferred financial growth in those accounts, which is one of the key benefits of having a retirement account in the first place.

"You'd have to be in an extreme emergency to ever do it," Smith says. "People are really going to be paying the price if they get to retirement and don't have what they need to get through that period of life."

It's important to do research, but it also matters where that information is coming from. While social media platforms like TikTok have made financial literacy more accessible to a younger generation, they have also made it easier to spread financial misinformation and to mislead investors.

A 2023 study published by the Swiss Finance Institute found low accuracy levels in the advice offered by financial influencers, often called "finfluencers." In an analysis of 29,000 finfluencers, researchers found that

28% provided valuable investment advice, while the majority (56%) were characterized as "antiskilled" because they gave investment advice that led to negative returns on average in comparison to the market at large.

"Surprisingly, unskilled and antiskilled finfluencers have more followers, more activity, and more influence on retail trading than skilled finfluencers," the researchers concluded. "As long as there are any antiskilled finfluencers 'preaching' their message, the investors tend to like their message and are willing to trade on it."

That conclusion is a cautionary tale for investors about the prevalence of low-quality financial advice floating around on the internet. The lesson: Make sure you're taking advice from reliable sources, and don't do something just to follow a friend, family member, or influencer.

"Don't invest in an asset just because your best friend is doing it," Rhinehart says.

8 MANAGE YOUR RISK

Scott says figuring out how to manage risk is the "the most important question of all," and it's what everyone should focus on as they start their investing journey.

Risk tolerance—the level of risk and potential loss someone is comfortable with—varies significantly.

A person's age, goals, and investing timeline—when they plan to withdraw their money—affect their risk tolerance. Generally, investors who are older and closer to retirement will need to take a less risky strategy because they're operating on a shorter timeline and will have less time to recover any potential losses. Investors with a longer timeline—young people saving for retirement, for example—can afford to make more risky investments because they have more time to recover.

Investors fall into three broad categories of risk: aggressive, moderate, and conservative. Aggressive investors are the most comfortable with risks, willing to take big ones in the hopes of seeing big rewards, even if it means weathering the steep highs and lows of market fluctuations. Moderate investors are less comfortable with risk but are willing to tolerate some losses while pursuing moderate gains. Conservative investors are the least risk-tolerant, seeking out investments that are more stable even though they are likely to yield lower results.

When figuring out where they stand on the risk-tolerance scale, Scott advises people to ask themselves, "What is it that I'm risking?"

"If I invest this money, and it drops 45%, what's the impact to my lifestyle going to be?" Scott says. "And if the impact to your lifestyle is going to be severe, then that means you've got to find something less risky."

However, being too risk-averse can lead to missed financial opportunities.

"Over time, not being invested is exponentially harmful because you miss out on so much compounding," says Preston Cherry, president of Concurrent Financial Planning and director of the Charles Schwab Foundation Center for Financial Wellness at the University of Wisconsin, Green Bay. He encourages people to examine why they're risk-averse and challenges that aversion with education, teaching about the power of investing over time.

"Your risk-averseness may keep you from achieving your goals," he says. "How would you feel if your life and money goals came up short because of not investing over time?"

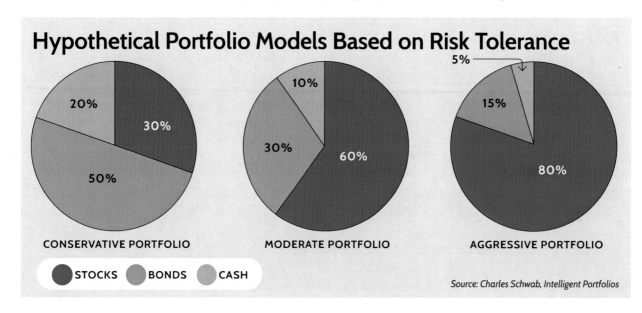

Hypothetical Portfolio Models Based on Risk Tolerance

CONSERVATIVE PORTFOLIO
30%, 50%, 20%

MODERATE PORTFOLIO
60%, 30%, 10%

AGGRESSIVE PORTFOLIO
80%, 15%, 5%

STOCKS BONDS CASH

Source: Charles Schwab, Intelligent Portfolios

9 BE A TAX-EFFICIENT INVESTOR

Being tax-efficient means paying the least amount of taxes required by law. It's important for investors to be mindful of tax rates, which differ depending on the asset and the type of income.

One of the best tax-efficient strategies is investing in your employer's 401(k) or similar retirement program. If your employer matches a percentage of your contribution to your retirement fund, try to contribute the maximum amount that your employer will match to make the most of that benefit. "The money you put away will be tax-deferred, so you won't have to pay income taxes on it in this current period," Smith says.

When you eventually make withdrawals from any tax-deferred investments, including IRAs and 401(k)s, they will incur regular income taxes. If you withdraw money from either plan before age 59½, the money will be subject to an additional 10% tax penalty. (Withdrawals from Roth IRAs are not taxed because contributions are made after taxes.)

Profits from the sale of an asset are taxed differently and are subject to a capital gains tax. The tax rate depends on how long you've owned the stock. If you sell an asset after owning it for a year or less, that profit is considered a short-term capital gain. Profits from assets owned for more than a year are considered long-term capital gains and are subject to a lower tax rate. That's why there's a benefit to holding stocks for a long period of time, rather than constantly buying and selling as day traders do.

"The people that get in trouble with taxable accounts are the people that are constantly buying and selling," Silberstein says. "That's what causes potential short-term gains, or potential tax implications that they might have not expected."

Most U.S. capital gains are subject to a long-term tax rate of 15%. That applies if your taxable income falls between $41,675 and $459,750 for single tax-filers. People who exceed that threshold—single people making more than $459,750 and married couples making more than $517,200—will face a capital gains tax rate of 20%. In Canada, only 50% of total capital gains is taxable. Meanwhile, if a single person's taxable income is less than or equal to $41,675 and a married couple's taxable income is less than or equal to $83,350, they won't have to pay taxes on capital gains.

Both mutual funds and ETFs are subject to capital gains taxes and taxes on dividends, which are earnings passed on to shareholders, typically at the end of the year. But ETFs are known for being more tax efficient, largely because they rarely pay out capital gains. So ETF investors are rarely subject to capital gains taxes until they sell their ETF and turn a profit.

Mutual fund distributions are reported to shareholders at the end of the calendar year on IRS Form 1099-DIV and count as investment income on a person's annual taxes. But the type of investment and type of distribution affect how much you'll owe in taxes.

Tax-loss harvesting is one strategy investors can use to minimize capital gains tax liability. If an investor loses money on the sale of an asset, they can use that loss to offset capital gains and lower the amount of taxes they will owe. For example, if someone made $20,000 in long-term capital gains from the sale of an asset but lost $5,000 on the sale of another, they would owe capital gains taxes on $15,000 instead.

"When you find yourself holding on to a loser, hoping it's coming back, and it's not, sometimes it's just best to say 'Hey, this one didn't work out. Let me take my losses,'" Smith says. "You can use those losses to offset gains."

10

SET IT, DON'T FORGET IT

Automating your investments—setting up regular contributions from your paycheck or bank account—is a great way to form an investing habit and stay consistent. It also ensures that you won't be tempted to use that money for something that's not a necessity, or make an excuse about not wanting to invest that month.

But financial advisors also recommend that you stay aware of what your investing strategy is and whether it needs to change.

"Automate, but don't go on autopilot," Silberstein says, noting that a person's financial goals might change, so it's important to pay attention to your investment strategy and make sure it matches your goals. "Especially over a 30- to 35-year period, you're not the same person. There's going to be six different versions of you, and six different versions of your investment strategy."

There are many options for online brokers—from Fidelity to TD Ameritrade to Charles Schwab—through which you can manage your portfolio and trade stocks, bonds, and mutual funds.

Silberstein recommends choosing the broker that you're most comfortable with and that fits your financial goals. Look for reliability, ease of access, user-friendly technology, and good customer service. You can also compare the account fees and commissions charged by different brokers, as well as their required account minimum. Many major online brokers now require no account minimum and offer no-fee trading on stocks and ETFs.

Some more experienced investors might need more complex advice and assistance from a financial advisor, but especially for people who are just beginning their investing journey,

there are plenty of low-cost online brokers that will be easily able to meet their needs.

"Does everyone need a financial advisor? No," Silberstein says. "But does everyone deserve ethical financial advice? Absolutely."

And while paying attention to your portfolio and investment strategy is important, you also don't want to overdo it.

Look at the monthly or quarterly statement from your brokerage firm, and consider rebalancing your portfolio maybe once per year. But also resist the urge to constantly check your portfolio to see how your investments are performing.

"Some people stress over watching the market every day, saying, 'Oh my account's down X amount of dollars,'" Smith says. "That kind of daily roller-coaster ride is totally unnecessary."

THE BOTTOM LINE

Investing is an essential step in building the future you want for yourself, and the best thing you can do is start now. Take advantage of the "magic of compounding" by investing early and allowing your portfolio to grow over the long term. Build a balanced portfolio that will help you weather market fluctuations. Make automated investment contributions, but stay informed about what you're investing in and when you might need to make adjustments. And manage the level of risk you take on by doing research through reputable sources and building a diversified portfolio with a combination of assets that feels comfortable for you. Don't expect to see instant results or to make perfect investing decisions, but keep your long-term goals in mind.

"I typically tell new investors this: It takes courage to get in the game, commitment to stay in the game, and consistency to win the game," Rhinehart says. "That's how you build a portfolio that provides the lifestyle you want for the rest of your life." ⓩ

TIP

An annual portfolio review is a good time to check investment performance, decide if rebalancing is needed, and see how you're tracking toward goals.

ASK THE EXPERTS

What Are Your Top Investing Rules?

Essential guidelines 10 pros swear by

BY ERIN GOBLER

A s with countless other endeavors, when you're getting started with investing, it helps to learn from the experts. Even if you choose to manage your own portfolio, getting advice from professionals can help take your investing success to the next level.

To help you on your investing journey, we spoke with 10 financial experts from Investopedia's 100 Top Financial Advisors of 2023 to get their best investing rules. These tips go beyond the standard advice about diversifying your portfolio and investing for the long term; they get to the root of the mindset you need to be a successful investor.

MICHAEL KITCES
Head of Planning Strategy, Buckingham Strategic Wealth

When you're in the first half of your career—your 20s and 30s and perhaps even early 40s—the best investment you can make is not in something popular like a tax-free Roth for growth. It's making an investment in yourself and your ability to earn more income.

[That] is the time to earn more money with a higher salary, so the earlier you are in your career, the more this pays off; the strategy diminishes in value over time as your career time horizon gets shorter. For those in their 20s and 30s, the wealth impact of investing in yourself and your career far outweighs traditional investing if you can get any level of raise as a result.

ELAINE KING
Founder, Family and Money Matters Institute

My top investing rule is to invest in things that align with your personal values. For example, several of my clients favor companies that are environmentally friendly and [may] pass on potential gains from [other] companies that may give them a higher return. These clients not only talk about being green, but they are also green at home, at work, and socially.

This way of thinking mostly benefits those who have identified their purpose and want to focus on it in all ways possible—personally, professionally, and socially. In my case, it is financial education. I started to align my actions to my purpose in my mid-20s, and I am still working on it.

DOUGLAS BONEPARTH
President, Bone Fide Wealth, LLC

Many people suggest that you should start investing "right now." This sentiment is mostly driven by the effects of compounding returns, because the sooner you can get money invested, the sooner you can start compounding your wealth. But often missing from this equation is that for investors to compound their returns, they need to stay invested over the long term. However, life isn't a straight line, and even our best intentions get challenged by both our own behaviors and a slew of external factors.

I use a rule called "earning the right to invest." This means that before you invest your hard-earned money, you first put yourself in a position to stay invested by mastering your cash flow and building a robust cash reserve. It's OK to spend time establishing a strong financial foundation before investing if it means you get to stay in the game longer.

MARGUERITA CHENG
Chief Executive Officer, Blue Ocean Global Wealth

My rule is that it's always a good time to invest, even when you're young. I helped my daughter open her Roth IRA when she was 15, and when she hit her first $500, I started matching her contributions. Teens, young students, and young professionals can all be successful investors. You don't have to invest the maximum amount, but I don't want young people to miss the opportunity for tax-free growth for their future. It doesn't have to be about retirement but about wealth accumulation for your future.

STEPHANIE McCULLOUGH
Founder & Financial Planner, Sofia Financial

The first step in investing is always to ask yourself, "Should this money actually be invested?"

Only long-term money should be invested because of the risks inherent in it. Investments go up and down in value at unpredictable rates and times. There is a place for cash in everyone's financial picture. This rule became clear to me in my conversations with clients over the years. So many people express frustration, saying, "I have this money in the bank earning nothing!" They forget about the benefits of cash, which never goes down in value during a crisis and is available at a moment's notice when the sh-t hits the fan.

PRESTON CHERRY
Founder & President, Concurrent Financial

"Life and money alignment gives money assignments."

According to Cherry's investing rule, you can find your ideal investment allocation by aligning your money with your life stage or priorities. For example, Cherry points to someone in their wealth-building stage with a high income whose priority is to accelerate their financial freedom:

"They may diversify across investment account types but only a little across investment types," he says. "They may accept higher market risk and concentration in domestic individual stock or index fund equities to help secure their life and money alignment. Their money has an investing style assignment that aligns with their life and money aspirations."

CAROLYN McCLANAHAN
Founder, Life Planning Partners, Inc.

Create an investment policy for yourself and stick to it! The market and the world are unpredictable, and crazy times play into our emotions about investments. By having an investment policy based on your goals, time frame, and ability to take risks, you can tune out the noise of the world and not make emotional mistakes with your portfolio.

Everyone needs the touchstone of an investment policy for their investments. Sticking with the plan through the 2009 crash, the pandemic crash, and all the times when the market went up, up, up has served my clients, and my own portfolio, very well. And the best part? You don't have to worry about all the craziness going on in the world—at least in relation to your investments.

REBECCA WALSER
Principal, Walser Wealth Management

The "psychology of the sunk investment," while it is simple, is the one thing even the best advisor on planet earth cannot overcome, regardless of how good they are. It is the dreaded "I want to wait until [this investment] gets back to [a given] amount to recapture some of the previous growth I've now lost."

While we can never disengage our emotions completely—because money is so integral and personal to our lives—we can be up front about expectations and run the management of risk-on assets in a more business-like fashion than one guided by gut feelings. So if you find yourself saying, "I'll sell this once it gets back to $XYZ," you probably want to check yourself, recognize the psychology of what is happening, and avoid holding out for a recovery that the analysis shows just isn't coming yet.

TAYLOR SCHULTE
Founder & CEO, Define Financial

Don't let the tax tail wag the investment dog. In other words, don't continue to hold an investment that doesn't align with your goals just because there is a tax consequence [if you] make a change. Similarly, investors should be cautious about buying an investment just because of a perceived tax benefit.

For example, a client of mine recently retired with 50% of her retirement nest egg invested in highly appreciated company stock. Naturally, she was hesitant about selling a large portion of the stock and paying capital gains taxes as a result. Through our conversations, we helped her recognize that maintaining a large, concentrated position exposed her retirement plan to significant risk—risk that she couldn't afford to take. In the end, she sold most of the stock, diversified the proceeds, and properly aligned the portfolio with her long-term goals.

PETER LAZAROFF
Chief Investment Officer, Plancorp

Losses are a necessary part of investing. Rather than try to predict when the market will fall and make portfolio moves based on those predictions—a process that research conclusively shows is a bad approach—you should plan on losses occurring with a similar magnitude and frequency as they have in the past. ⓔ

THE Investopedia Express
with Caleb Silver

Where educated investors get smart, and stay smart, about the markets, the economy, and their money.

SUBSCRIBE NOW · APPLE PODCASTS · SPOTIFY · GOOGLE PODCASTS · PLAYERFM

Never sell because of emotions.

Only invest in what you know about, and if you don't know enough about something and want to invest, do research and learn all you can before investing.

Hold for the long term.

A good investment in a bad market is massive opportunity.

Have patience!

Investopedia Readers Weigh In

From rules to live by to the best advice, we asked our readers what they think

Never underestimate the power of compounding.

Investopedia's millions of readers come to us from all over the world and with varying levels of financial knowledge. From seasoned investors to those just starting their investing journey, everyone has their own style when it comes to strategy and rules they follow.

So as we dive into our own rules of investing, we thought we'd ask our readers: What investing rules do you live by, and what's the best investing advice you've ever received? From Vancouver, Canada to New York City and everywhere in between, these are the words Investopedia readers live by when making decisions about their investments. ⮑

Invest in yourself.

Cash and patience are both positions.

The losses you've made are the price paid to learn. You won't get that at Uni.

An investment in education is the best investment.

Buy low, sell high.

Do not give into FOMO— invest within your means.

Think of investing as a marathon, not a sprint. The earlier you start investing, the more time your money has to grow.

Start now!

Always do your own due diligence.

SCAN HERE

Join the Instagram conversation and get quick tips, news digests, and more. Follow us @investopedia.

Apply the Rules

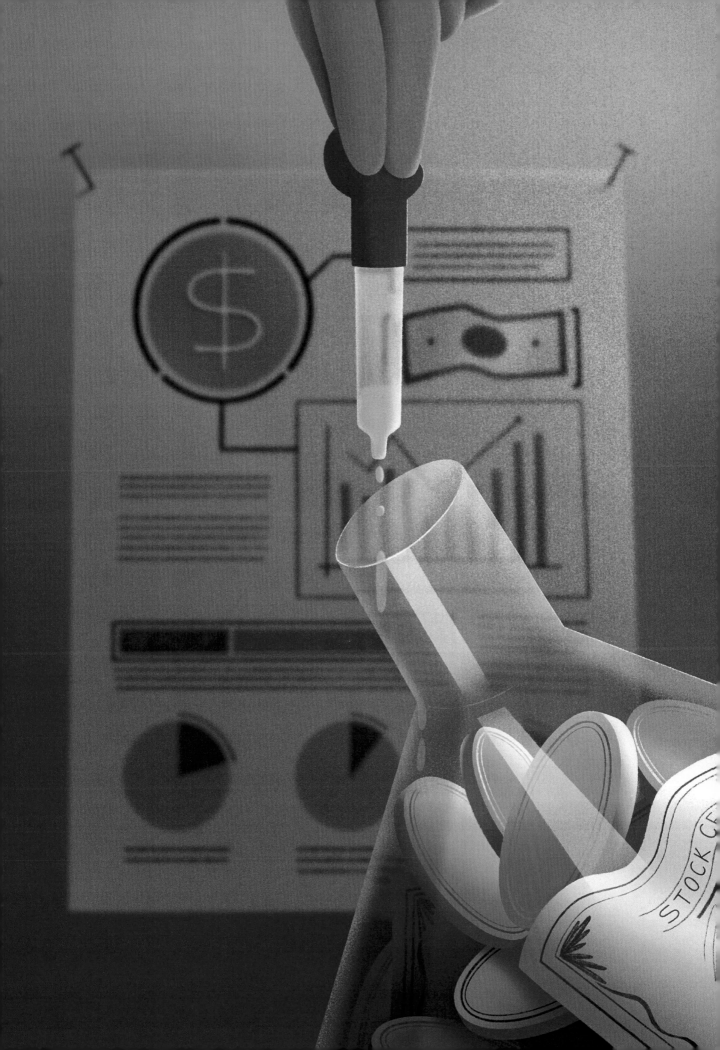

STOCKS · ETFS · BONDS · INDEX FUNDS

Wise Ways To Invest in Stocks

Enjoy the rewards and reduce the risks by following these basic guidelines

BY GREG DAUGHERTY

When you buy a share of stock, you're essentially purchasing a piece of a corporation, often a very tiny piece—Apple Inc., for example, has more than 15 billion shares outstanding. If the company does well, you stand to profit. If it does poorly, you could lose money, possibly every cent you've invested.

So stocks can be risky, but they can also be rewarding. The S&P 500 Stock Index, which tracks 500 leading U.S. companies, was up an average of 10.71% for the 10-year period ending September 1, 2023. By comparison, the S&P 500 Bond Index rose at an average rate of 2.66% a year over the same period.

Impressive average stock returns like that tend to gloss over some wild

FAST FACT

More than 2,300 public companies are listed on the New York Stock Exchange (NYSE).

ups and downs, however. In 2021, for example, the S&P 500 rose more than 23% for the year, then dropped 18% in 2022. For that reason, most financial advisors see stocks as a long-term investment—and the rest of us probably should, too.

TYPES OF STOCKS

There are two basic types of stocks: common and preferred. Common stocks, the more widely held of the two, come with voting rights, allowing the shareholder to vote yay or nay on the company's board of directors and other matters.

Preferred stocks, on the other hand, don't come with voting rights. Their potential advantage is that they typically pay dividend income, while common stocks, even of the same company, may not. In addition, if a company goes bankrupt, preferred shareholders have a better chance of getting at least some of their money back than their common-shareholder counterparts.

Within those two types of stocks, there are also a variety of subcategories. One distinction many investors draw is between growth stocks and value stocks.

Growth stocks represent companies whose share price has the potential for significant appreciation. These are usually new and smaller companies, today often in the tech and e-commerce sectors. Growth stocks generally don't pay dividends, instead plowing that money back into the business. People who invest in them are hoping that their share price will rise enough to return a solid profit.

Value stocks are more conservative. They're likely to rise in price more slowly but to provide a reliable flow of dividends. Examples today are often in sectors such as banking, consumer staples, and the oil industry.

Many investors also look for value stocks that are undervalued, meaning that their share price underestimates their true worth. This is how the legendary investor Warren Buffett became one of the richest people in the world.

For investors without the stock-picking gifts of a Warren Buffett, advisors generally recommend building a diversified portfolio with a mix of both growth and value stocks.

STOCKS AND YOUR PORTFOLIO

While stocks can be an important part of your portfolio, other kinds of investments will come in handy, too—especially if stocks are down for an extended period and you need to get some money out. You might want to buy a new car, for example, or put a down payment on a house.

Many experts, including Louis Baraja, a certified financial planner in Irvine, Calif., and one of Investopedia's 100 Top Financial Advisors of 2023, suggest thinking of your portfolio in terms of cash, fixed income, and equity.

Cash isn't just greenbacks but readily available funds in places like bank accounts; they may not earn a lot, but they probably won't to lose anything, either. Fixed income refers to bonds and bond mutual funds, rarely big profit-makers but pretty stable. Equities, finally, is another name for stocks and stock funds.

What percentage of your money to put in each will depend on factors like your age, how soon you plan to retire, and how much risk you're comfortable with. As a general rule, the younger you are, the more risk you can afford to take, so the more money you might consider putting in stocks. But even older investors

---

IMPORTANT

Some stocks pay shareholder dividends, the distribution of corporate earnings to eligible sharedholders. Dividends are typically paid out quarterly in cash or as additional stock reinvestments.

Looking at the Market Through a 50-Year Lens

This chart compares annual volatility to a rolling 15-year return average, showing the long-term growth that can come from staying invested through downturns and corrections.

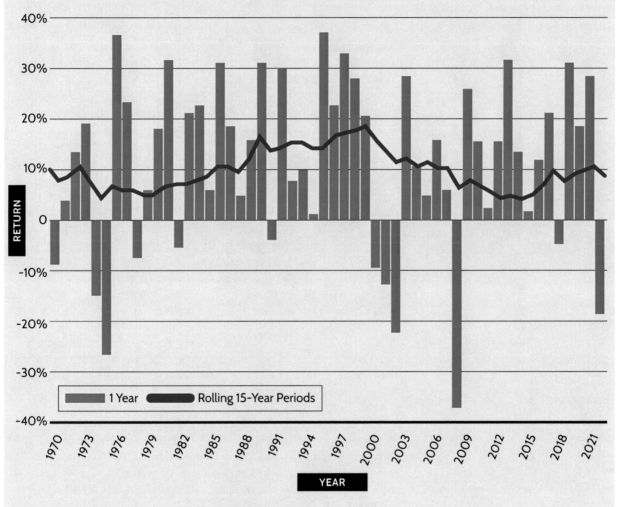

Sources: T. Rowe Price, created with Zephyr StyleADVISOR, and S&P. Price return calculations include dividends and capital gains. Annual returns and rolling 15-year data began in calendar year 1970.

usually want to keep some money in stocks, since these days retirement can last for several decades.

"If you leave all your money for the next 25 years in a savings account, that's the riskiest investment you can have, because it's at the mercy of inflation," Barajas notes.

HOW TO INVEST IN STOCKS
While a few companies sell their shares directly to the public, you'll generally need a brokerage account to buy stocks. These days, online $0 trade fee brokers are prevalent, while traditional full-service brokers are more costly but also offer advice on which stocks to consider and which to avoid.

Whether or not you're relying on a broker's recommendations, it's usually best to focus on companies you know and whose products you understand. Resist the impulse to act on a tip from "somebody at the car wash or your brother-in-law at the Labor Day barbecue," Barajas cautions.

Similarly, Randy Carver, president and CEO of Carver Financial Services in Mentor, Ohio, advises against buying stock on the basis of the latest headlines. "By then it's probably too late," he says. "It will already have gone up."

If you don't have the time or

inclination to research individual stocks, an alternative is to invest in mutual funds or exchange-traded funds (ETFs). They hold a diversified portfolio of stocks, avoiding the risks inherent in any single company. And when, if ever, should you consider selling? Even buy-and-hold diehards suggest a couple of scenarios. One, of course, is if you need the money for other purposes. Another is if you set a price target going in and the stock has now exceeded it.

Perhaps most important: if there's been a fundamental change in the company (its management, its strategy, its position in the marketplace) that now makes it a stock you wouldn't have bought in the first place.

APPLYING THE RULES
Consider these three solid suggestions for what to do now:

Start Now!
Because stocks are a long-term proposition, the sooner you get started, the better off you'll be. If you can regularly invest a portion of your paycheck, you'll also benefit from dollar-cost averaging: Your money will buy fewer shares when prices are high but more when they dip, resulting in a lower average cost per share.

If you own dividend-paying stocks and don't need the cash for everyday expenses, you can enroll in a dividend reinvestment plan, which will use it to buy more shares each quarter. Many companies offer these plans, as do brokerage firms.

Nancy Tengler, the author of *The Women's Guide to Successful Investing* and the CEO and chief investment officer at Laffer Tengler Investments in Scottsdale, Ariz., points out that dividend reinvestment plans will not only build your stock holdings, but, because they're automatic, they also enjoy the advantage of dollar-cost averaging.

Time Is Everything
Financial pros will tell you that market-timing—knowing exactly when to buy low and sell high—is virtually impossible. But timing of another sort does play a critical role in stock investing. That's your time horizon.

"If you buy quality companies, they should go up over time," Carver says. "But that's assuming at least a three- to five-year time frame, not a three-week time frame. If you can't wait that long, you shouldn't be in the market."

Barajas agrees, noting that personal goals can also affect the time frame. "If you're cutting a college tuition check in a year, you probably don't want to have that money in stocks," he says. "If your time horizon is retirement, and it's 15 years away, that's a different story."

Tame Your Animal Spirits
"The biggest mistakes in investing are behavioral," Barajas says, "driven by greed or fear." Even investors who aren't particularly greedy can easily succumb to fear, bailing out in a panic when the overall market or a certain stock they own takes a tumble.

"For the average investor, large companies that have brand and market share usually figure out how to solve their problems," Tengler says. "That's how you create wealth—stay in and reinvest those dividends."

Plenty of data bear that out. For example, the Baltimore-based investment firm T. Rowe Price compared the likely returns of a hypothetical "steady investor" to an

SCAN HERE

Check out Investopedia's roundup of the best online stock trading platforms.

2 in 3 Investors Pick Stocks for Best 10-Year Returns

A September 2023 survey of Investopedia readers found that investors think U.S. stocks will deliver the best returns over the next decade.

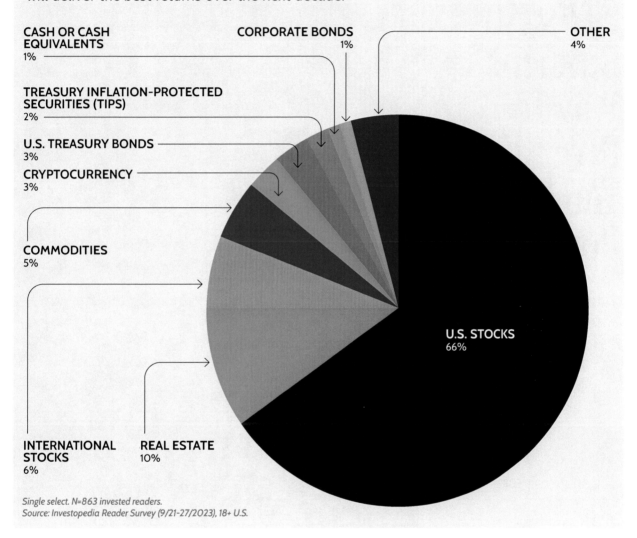

CASH OR CASH EQUIVALENTS
1%

TREASURY INFLATION-PROTECTED SECURITIES (TIPS)
2%

U.S. TREASURY BONDS
3%

CRYPTOCURRENCY
3%

COMMODITIES
5%

CORPORATE BONDS
1%

OTHER
4%

U.S. STOCKS
66%

INTERNATIONAL STOCKS
6%

REAL ESTATE
10%

Single select. N=863 invested readers.
Source: Investopedia Reader Survey (9/21-27/2023), 18+ U.S.

"anxious investor" from 2001 through 2022, a period that included the global financial crisis of 2007-2008.

The steady investor stayed in the market and continued to make regular contributions, while the anxious one jumped in and out based on the financial news. In the end, the steady investor would have come away with more than twice as much money as their anxious peer.

THE BOTTOM LINE

Despite their potential risks, stocks have proven to be one of the most reliable ways to build wealth over time. Whether you're a new investor or a seasoned one, certain fundamentals stand out: Know what you're buying and why.

Plan to hang in for the long haul, unless you have a logical reason for selling. And try to keep your emotions in check—although there's no harm in feeling a little pleased with yourself as you watch your portfolio grow. ℮

STOCKS   **ETFS**   BONDS   INDEX FUNDS

ETFs: An Efficient Way To Diversify Your Portfolio

Powerful tools for many different investing strategies

BY NATHAN REIFF

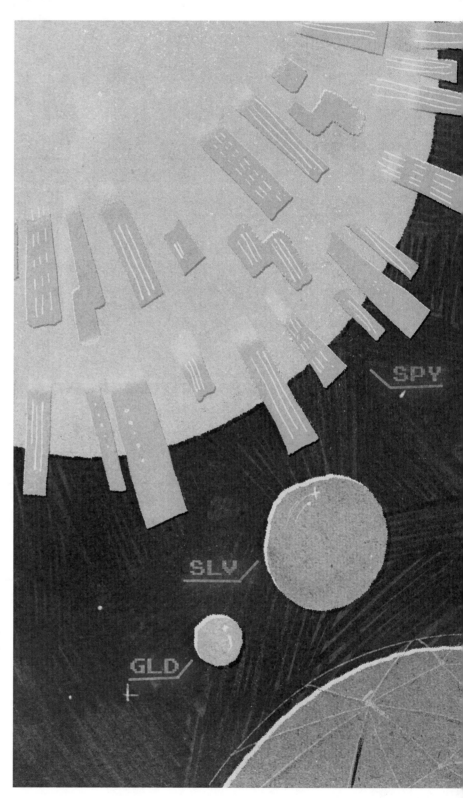

Since exchange-traded funds (ETFs) began to trade in the U.S. 30 years ago, they have emerged as one of the most popular and readily accessible investment vehicles.

ETFs take much of the work of managing a diversified portfolio out of the hands of investors, placing this burden instead in the hands of fund managers or, increasingly, in automated systems. In exchange, investors pay a modest fee called an expense ratio to the ETF provider to

participate in owning shares of the fund, which trade throughout the day like stocks.

There are thousands of different ETFs, each providing exposure to a basket of stocks, a commodity, or another asset or group of assets.

Funds exist for a host of different themes and specializations, allowing investors to target everything from companies involved in the blockchain space and names in particular geographic regions to companies focused on environmental, social, and corporate governance ideals, and those comprising popular indices like the S&P 500 or the Nasdaq. This is one reason why Charlene Rhinehart, CPA, PMP, likens ETFs to "going to a mall where you can find a variety of options in one place."

While getting into the world of ETFs is easy for investors of all kinds, making the most of these powerful tools—and knowing which pose a level of risk unmanageable for your portfolio—can be difficult.

WHAT IS AN ETF?

ETFs operate similarly to mutual funds in that they pool investor assets to invest in a particular sector, index, group of securities, or commodity. They differ from mutual and index funds both in terms of the breadth of areas of focus and, crucially, because shares of ETFs are traded on stock exchanges like individual stocks.

Some of the most popular funds include the SPDR S&P 500 ETF Trust (SPY), the first ETF and still among the most liquid, which targets the S&P 500; the Invesco QQQ Trust (QQQ), which tracks the Nasdaq-100 Index; and the Vanguard Total Stock Market ETF (VTI), which aims to provide exposure to the entire U.S. stock market.

One of the benefits of ETFs—

the ability to easily add diversification to a portfolio without having to select individual stocks—makes ETFs a "great choice for amateur investors," says Luis Rosa, CFP, creator of the "On My Way to Wealth" podcast. Another benefit is easy access to specialized investment strategies, including those employing leverage and shorting tools. And ETFs are generally managed passively, which helps to keep annual fees down.

They also come with risks, however, including no guarantee of returns, an inability for investors to specify which securities or other assets are included in the portfolio, and, in some cases, low liquidity, which makes trading difficult and expensive.

ETFS AND YOUR PORTFOLIO

ETFs can be a part of a well-balanced, diversified portfolio. Because ETFs exist to focus on a huge variety of investment areas, many investors may be tempted to populate their portfolio exclusively with these funds. However, Rhinehart cautions against including only ETFs in your portfolio, saying that "the [combined] annual fees...can eat into your investment return over time."

When considering ETFs for investment, consider the following:
• Level of risk
• Match between the ETF and your investment strategy
• Expense ratio of the ETF

To evaluate the risk level of the fund, consider a risk rating from an independent financial-services company like Morningstar, or look to past performance and the degree to which a fund deviates from its mean returns. Some ETFs, and particularly those employing leverage or other complex investment strategies, may carry high levels of risk.

FAST FACT

By 2027, ETFs will account for 24% of total fund assets, up from 17% in 2023.

The ETF Market Is Booming

As of December 2022, the total size of the U.S. and Europe ETF market is approximately $6.7 trillion assets under management, led by a sharp rise in active ETFs. Overall, the landscape can be differentiated by four main strategies: purely passive, smart beta, thematic, and purely active.

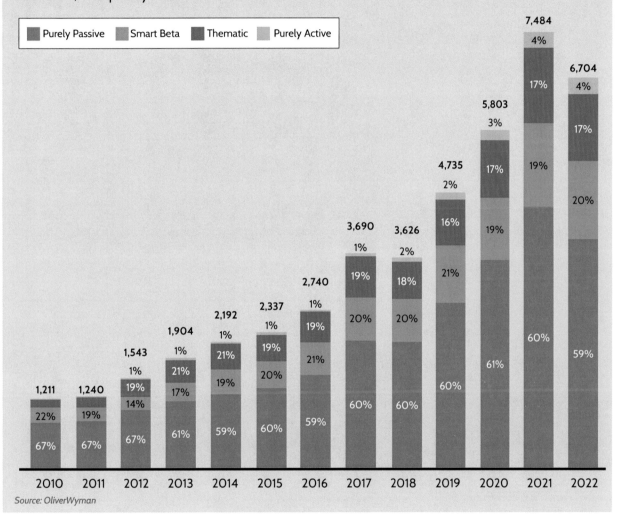

Legend: Purely Passive | Smart Beta | Thematic | Purely Active

Year	Total	Purely Active	Thematic	Smart Beta	Purely Passive
2010	1,211			22%	67%
2011	1,240			19%	67%
2012	1,543	1%	19%	14%	67%
2013	1,904	1%	21%	17%	61%
2014	2,192	1%	21%	19%	59%
2015	2,337	1%	19%	20%	60%
2016	2,740	1%	19%	21%	59%
2017	3,690	1%	19%	20%	60%
2018	3,626	2%	18%	20%	60%
2019	4,735	2%	16%	21%	60%
2020	5,803	3%	17%	19%	61%
2021	7,484	4%	17%	19%	60%
2022	6,704	4%	17%	20%	59%

Source: OliverWyman

It's also essential to take into account your investment strategy and how it matches with the profile of a particular fund. Not all ETFs are good for buy-and-hold investors. Indeed, some funds—including leveraged funds, mentioned previously—are typically designed for active investors who buy and sell them within a single trading day.

An example of a popular leveraged ETF is the ProShares Ultra QQQ Fund (QLD). Like QQQ, QLD targets the Nasdaq-100 Index. However, QLD is designed to provide daily returns equal to twice those of the index. Investors holding the fund for longer periods may be subject to distorted returns.

Another crucial element to consider in an ETF is the expense ratio, or annual fee. Expense ratios constitute the fee that holders of a fund pay to the fund manager. Many funds, particularly very popular ones such as SPY, traditionally carry quite low expense ratios.

For example, the Vanguard S&P 500 ETF (VOO) has an expense ratio of just 0.03%. However, other funds, including actively-managed ETFs and specialized vehicles like the Breakwave Dry Bulk Shipping ETF

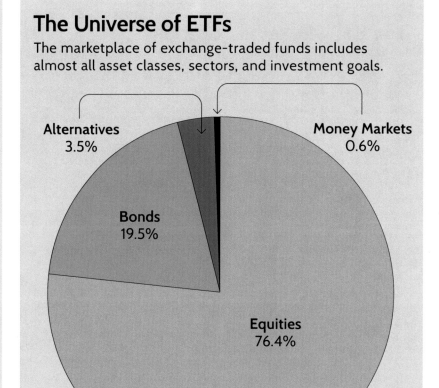

The Universe of ETFs

The marketplace of exchange-traded funds includes almost all asset classes, sectors, and investment goals.

Alternatives
3.5%

Money Markets
0.6%

Bonds
19.5%

Equities
76.4%

Source: BlackRock iShares

FAST FACT

There's an ETF for almost anything—even an Inverse Cramer ETF for traders who want to do the opposite of what TV personality Jim Cramer does, such as short-selling his buy recommendations or buying his sell recommendations.

(BDRY), may have much higher fees (in the case of BDRY, 2.85%). Beginners to the ETF space or those looking to minimize costs may be best served looking at inexpensive passively-managed funds.

HOW TO INVEST IN ETFS

There are many effective ways to invest in ETFs beyond a simple buy-and-hold approach. Here are a few of the most common strategies:

Asset Allocation

Investors considering asset allocation—diversifying their portfolio across a number of different asset classes—may flock to ETFs because they provide a simple way of accessing this broad diversification. Different ETFs can help investors focus on stocks, bonds, commodities, and other asset types, allowing for sweeping variety in each category or a highly targeted approach.

Sector Rotation

Looking to capitalize on shifting trends on a sector-wide level?

Specialized ETFs focusing on sector-specific indices, such as the Energy Select Sector SPDR Fund (XLE) or the iShares U.S. Real Estate ETF (IYR), make it easy to quickly enter or exit a position targeting a particular sector.

Dollar-Cost Averaging

One of the most popular investment approaches for amateur investors, dollar-cost averaging (the technique of buying a fixed amount of a particular asset on a regular basis to account, over time, for variations in the price of the asset) works especially well with ETFs because they are traded as easily as stocks.

Short Selling

Savvy investors looking to short a particular industry, sector, geographic area, and so on will often turn to ETFs to make a bet that is larger in scope than shorting a single stock.

APPLYING THE RULES

Investopedia's rules of investing apply to ETFs of all kinds. Here are some of the most important:

Aim for Balance

ETFs can easily broaden and diversify your portfolio. Are you looking to expand your reach into bonds or into a particular part of the world or industry? It's virtually guaranteed that there's at least one ETF to cover it.

For amateur investors, ETF managers take care of the rebalancing part for you. On the other hand, this means that ETF investors don't have the opportunity to fine-tune a basket of stocks for their portfolio. But for those craving simplicity, ETFs are hard to beat.

Know What You Own (and Why You Own It)

A danger of ETFs is that an investor can buy up shares of a fund without knowing all of the fund's holdings. Not only can this lead to conflicts between portfolio makeup and investment ideals (an investor may unwittingly hold oil and gas stocks in a general large-cap fund, say, even if they wish to focus on environmental, social, and governance goals), but it also means investors may not pay attention to what's best for them.

There are times, after all, when it's best to be able to control the exact securities you own. In these scenarios, ETFs may not be the best option.

Manage Your Risk

While most ETFs are highly diversified, posing relatively less risk than investing an equivalent amount of money in a single stock, there are other funds carrying significant risk.

Besides leveraged, inverse, and other funds with complex strategies, some funds have relatively small baskets of holdings. Others may hold a number of stocks, say, but weigh just a few stocks such that they comprise the bulk of the portfolio.

In any of these cases, unexpected performance by even a single stock in an ETF's basket can jeopardize the performance of the entire fund.

THE BOTTOM LINE

ETFs make it easy for investors to broaden their exposure and balance out risk—at least when used properly. They offer powerful opportunities to fine-tune areas of focus in a portfolio while freeing investors from the work of buying and selling individual stocks or other assets.

Investing in ETFs shouldn't be a substitute for doing due diligence about companies, industries, and sectors that may be worth exploring or avoiding. Still, the broad usefulness of ETFs as tools for buy-and-hold investors, active traders, short sellers, dollar-cost average subscribers, and many other profiles helps explain their massive popularity over the last several decades.

SCAN HERE

Read more about the latest ETF news and market developments on *Investopedia.com*.

STOCKS — ETFS — BONDS — INDEX FUNDS

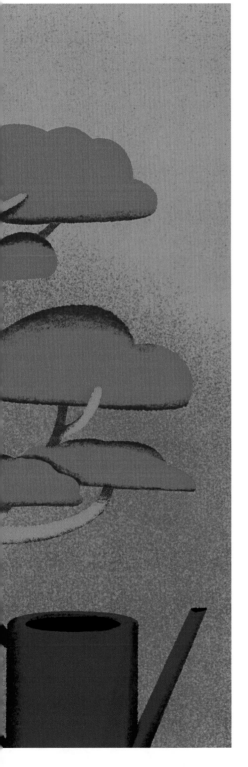

The Balancing Effect of Bonds

Bonds can be a steady, low-risk stream of income in your portfolio

BY KATIE REILLY

Bonds are a critical piece of any balanced investment portfolio. They can serve as an anchor that helps keep your portfolio steady when riskier investments fluctuate in value due to market volatility.

There's a lot to consider before you begin investing in bonds—how they work, what risks they carry, and what kind of returns you can expect. These are the basics that every investor should know.

WHAT IS A BOND?

A bond is a type of investment that generally carries less risk than stocks and offers a consistent source of income. Investing in a bond means lending money to a company or a government agency, which will pay back the money, along with a set amount of interest, after a certain period of time—known as the maturity date.

"A bond is a debt obligation, like an IOU," according to an explanation by

MAIN BOND CATEGORIES

▶ **CORPORATE BONDS**
Issued by companies as an alternative to seeking a bank loan for debt financing.

▶ **MUNICIPAL BONDS**
Issued by states and municipalities. Some municipal bonds offer tax-free coupon income for investors.

▶ **GOVERNMENT BONDS**
Bonds issued by a government treasury are often collectively referred to as treasuries. The U.S. Treasury issues bills, notes, and bonds, differentiated based on their rates of maturity. Government bonds issued by national governments may be referred to as sovereign debt.

▶ **AGENCY BONDS**
Issued by government-affiliated organizations such as Fannie Mae or Freddie Mac.

the Securities and Exchange Commission.

Types of bonds include corporate bonds, municipal bonds and government bonds, often called treasuries. Investors who buy bonds are effectively lending money to the company or government agency issuing the bond. In return, that entity pays the investor interest regularly and eventually repays the principal investment when the bond matures.

"This is really helpful for investors who are seeking predictable income payments. They can say, 'I know I'm gonna get this much money on this date,'" says Cody Garrett, a certified financial planner and owner of Measure Twice Financial in Houston.

The company or agency might use that loan to raise money for projects, such as acquiring new equipment; building roads, schools, and bridges; investing in research and development; and financing mergers and acquisitions.

Corporate bonds are issued by private and public companies. Municipal bonds are issued by states, cities, and other government bodies. Treasury bonds are backed by the U.S. government, which makes them one of the safest investments, but they also yield lower returns.

Risk

Bonds are generally considered to be a less risky investment than stocks, but they are typically less rewarding as well. And investing in bonds still carries some risks. If a bond issuer defaults, they might not be able to repay their debts, and bondholders could lose all their invested money.

Investors can assess risk by looking at a bond's credit rating from agencies, including Moody's, Standard & Poor's and Fitch. Investment-grade bonds have high credit ratings, meaning the agencies are more confident the issuer

will make interest payments and ultimately repay the loan.

Higher-risk bonds, often called "junk bonds," have a lower credit rating—typically BB+ or lower by Standard & Poor's and Fitch, and Ba1 or lower by Moody's—and have a higher risk of defaulting.

Returns

When you own a stock, you own a piece of a company and receive returns based on the success of that company in the stock market. In comparison, a bond is a small loan to a government agency or company—or an investment in that entity's debt—that will be paid back with interest at a later date, regardless of the company's performance in the stock market.

While investors pay a specific commission to brokers when they buy individual stocks or mutual funds, commissions are typically bundled into the price of an individual bond and are called mark-ups. The higher the mark-up, the lower the yield on your investment will be.

You might opt to invest in bonds over stocks if you are more risk-averse and want a steady stream of income. The majority of bonds have a maturity date that's set when the bond is issued, according to the Financial Industry Regulatory Authority (FINRA). On that date, the bond issuer fulfills its debt obligation to the bondholder by paying the final interest payment and the bond's face value, called par value.

Until the bond reaches maturity, bondholders receive a payout of the annual interest, or coupon. For example, according to FINRA, a bond with a par value of $1,000 and an annual interest rate of 4.5%, would receive an annual coupon of $45, or $22.50 twice a year.

A bond's coupon rate—or coupon yield—is the interest rate established when the bond is issued, and it stays the

Breaking Down Bond Ratings

Ratings are an assessment of a bond issuer's creditworthiness and are used to judge its riskiness. Ratings also influence the return: A lower rating requires a higher return on the bond in order to compensate for the added risk the investor is taking on.

MOODY'S	STANDARD & POOR'S	FITCH	GRADE	RISK
Aaa	AAA	AAA	Investment	Lowest Risk
Aa1/Aa2/Aa3 /A1/A2/A3	AA+/AA/AA-/ A+/A/A-	AA+/AA/AA-/ A+/A/A-	Investment	Low risk
Baa1/Baa2/ Baa3	BBB+/BBB/ BBB-	BBB+/BBB/ BBB-	Investment	Medium Risk
Ba1/Ba2/Ba3/ B1/B2/B3	BB+/BB/BB-/ B+/B/B-	BB+/BB/BB-/ B+/B/B-	Junk	Medium Risk
Caa1/Caa2/ Caa3/Ca	CCC+/CCC/ CCC-/CC/C	CCC+/CCC/ CCC-/CC/C	Junk	High Risk
C	SD/D	RD/D	In Default	Highest Risk

same until the bond reaches maturity.

If an investor holds a bond to maturity, the coupon yield will be their total yield on the bond. But if an investor wants to buy or sell a bond before it reaches maturity, then the current yield is what matters. The current yield is affected by the bond's current market price, and it is calculated by dividing the annual coupon payment by the bond's current market value.

If the price of a bond increases, the current yield falls, because if an investor buys the bond at that price, they would be paying more than it was originally worth but would still receive the same coupon rate each year.

On the flip side, if the price of the bond decreases and an investor buys the bond at a discount, the current yield would increase.

BONDS AND YOUR PORTFOLIO
Bonds help to diversify your investments and create a balanced portfolio, in part because they operate differently than stocks.

Thomas Catalano, a certified financial planner and an Investopedia Financial Review Board member, advises all of his clients to invest in a mix of stocks, also called equities, and bonds, which are fixed-income investments, depending on their age and their financial goals.

"Stocks are going to return more than bonds over time," Catalano says. "If you're a younger investor, you can afford to load up on more equities because your time horizon is further out than someone who's approaching retirement. A younger investor in their 20s or 30s might have a mix of 80% equity and 20% fixed-income."

As an investor approaches retirement, they might invest in a higher percentage of bonds and a lower percentage of stocks because they would have less time to recover financially from a big market downturn.

Garrett says a mix of bonds with different maturity timelines can also be key to balance. Maturity dates differ depending on the bond, with some corporate bonds maturing in less than three years and some government bonds maturing in 20 to 30 years.

"I always ask, 'What is the money for, and when do you expect to need the money?'" he explains. "If somebody says, 'I'm expecting to use this money within two years,' I immediately think, we want stability more than income right now. So I'm going to buy short-term, high-quality bonds."

IMPORTANT

Bond value is directly related to interest rates: When market interest rates rise, prices of fixed-rate bonds fall. Conversely, when interest rates fall, prices of fixed-rate bonds rise.

But if someone isn't planning on using the money for 10 years or more, they could look into intermediate-term or long-term bonds, which carry more risk but also offer a higher yield.

The Impact of Interest Rate Changes
There's also interest rate risk. As interest rates rise, bond prices fall, and vice versa. This matters if an investor wants to sell the bond before it reaches maturity. If interest rates rise, they won't be able to sell it for as much as they paid for it originally.

"Say you invested in a 5% bond today, and then the Fed raises [interest] rates again. Let's say it goes to 6%. The price of your bond is going to go down because it's just not as attractive anymore," Catalano says. "Why would I pay you, dollar for dollar, on a bond at 5% when I could go get a new one at 6%?"

Investors should also consider the bond rating. If bonds have a lower credit rating (BB+ or lower by Standard & Poor's and Fitch, and Ba1 or lower by Moody's), they are considered non-investment-grade, or junk bonds. And the market considers them more likely to default.

Such bonds are typically high-yield and high-risk, and experts say investors should think twice before investing in them. "It's like lending money to somebody with a low credit score," Garrett says. "That's effectively what you're doing by chasing high-yield bonds." Meanwhile, bonds with a rating at or above BBB- from Standard & Poor's and Fitch and Baa3 from Moody's are considered to be stronger, investment-grade bonds.

Some bonds are also "callable," which allows the issuer to pay back the principal of a bond before it matures, therefore stopping interest payments early.

Investing in bonds also carries an inflation risk—meaning the money you invest will have less purchasing power by the time you are paid back.

One way to mitigate that risk is by investing in short-term bonds. A longer-term bond will be more susceptible to risks because there are more chances for interest rates to rise and for inflation to increase over a longer period of time. "The longer you own the bond, the more you have to worry about inflation eroding that," Garrett says.

Inflation can affect the return on a bond investment, hindering the actual value of the return. For example, a 30-year U.S. Treasury bond was offering a 4.58% yield in September, but when adjusted for inflation, the federal government could only guarantee a return of 2.2% on a 30-year bond—half the projected rate of return.

HOW TO INVEST IN BONDS
Unlike stocks, which are publicly traded on a centralized market, most bonds have to be bought through brokers. U.S. Treasury bonds can be bought directly from the government in amounts ranging from $25 to $10,000. You can also buy or sell bonds from other investors.

Brokers and brokerage firms charge fees, which vary depending on the type of bond investment, and some require an initial minimum deposit.

You can also invest in bonds through mutual funds or exchange-traded funds (ETFs) made up of bonds. Investing in a bond fund can efficiently diversify your portfolio with a smaller investment, saving you the trouble of selecting individual bonds on your own. Bond funds are also professionally managed, which can simplify the process for the investor.

A bond's price is based on what investors are willing to pay for it. The price is heavily affected by interest rates—as interest rates rise, the price of existing bonds will fall, because

What To Consider When Buying Bonds

PROS	CONS
Receive income through the interest payments	Bonds pay out lower returns than stocks
Hold the bond to maturity and get all your principal back	Companies can default on your bonds
Profit if you resell the bond at a higher price	Bond yields can fall

investors will be more interested in buying new bonds that will offer them the opportunity for higher interest payments.

"As the Fed adjusts rates to deal with different pieces of the economy, you could see your bond price deteriorate," Catalano says. "If you need to access that money, there's a chance that you could wind up selling the bond at a loss because the price is going to go down."

The price of bonds also depends on the credit rating of the issuer; investors will pay more for a bond if they are confident the issuer won't default.

APPLYING THE RULES
Keeping the following strategies in mind will help you become a more savvy and successful bond investor:

Aim for Balance
Bonds can help add balance to your portfolio if you invest in a mix of stocks, bonds, and other asset classes. It's important not to put all your eggs in one basket, including bonds. If interest rates rise or inflation increases, threatening the value of your bonds, maintaining a balanced portfolio helps to mitigate that risk.

Manage Your Risk
Every investor is different, and every investor has a different risk-tolerance level. Bonds are generally a good investment for people who are less risk-tolerant, but that doesn't mean they're risk-free. Look for bonds with good credit ratings and short-term maturities to balance out any more risky investments you might take on.

Be a Tax-Efficient Investor
You'll pay taxes on the income from most bond investments, including capital gains. Income from U.S. Treasury bonds is not subject to state and local taxes, and most municipal bonds are exempt from federal income, state, and local taxes, which can make them a tax-efficient option.

THE BOTTOM LINE

Bonds can be a ballast against losses from riskier investments. When the value of stocks is plummeting, bonds can provide a steady source of income.

But investors still need to consider the potential risks, bond prices, their own financial goals, and the broader economic climate when deciding which bond investments are right for them.

Garrett says he always asks his clients, "What are you going to use the money for? When do you need the money? And why do you want to own bonds?" He goes on, "If the answer is income, stability, and diversification, then bonds can provide those three things." ⟳

STOCKS — ETFS — BONDS — **INDEX FUNDS**

How To Start Investing in Index Funds

Learn how these low-cost investments can fit into a balanced portfolio

BY NAFEESAH ALLEN

Index funds are an important component of building long-term wealth. Even Warren Buffet, one of the world's most successful investors, recommends low-cost index funds as part of an overall investment portfolio. But with so many investment vehicles on the market, it's important to understand what index funds are, how they work, and why they are worth investing in.

According to Aryeh Sheinbein, principal and founder of Results Advisory, index funds associated with the Nasdaq, Russell 2000, or Standard & Poor's 500 Index are an "important part of a balanced portfolio, particularly because they reduce the fee structure."

In comparison to other investment options, such as mutual funds, stocks, and exchange traded funds (ETFs), the objective of index funds, broadly speaking, is to beat the average rate of returns of the S&P 500 while keeping fees associated with managing the investment very low.

TIP

Always compare index fund expense ratios. They are often cheaper than actively managed funds.

Over 1 in 3 Readers Expect S&P Losses over the Next Six Months

According to a September 2023 survey of Investopedia newsletter readers, many investors are expecting lower returns for the U.S. stock market over the next six months.

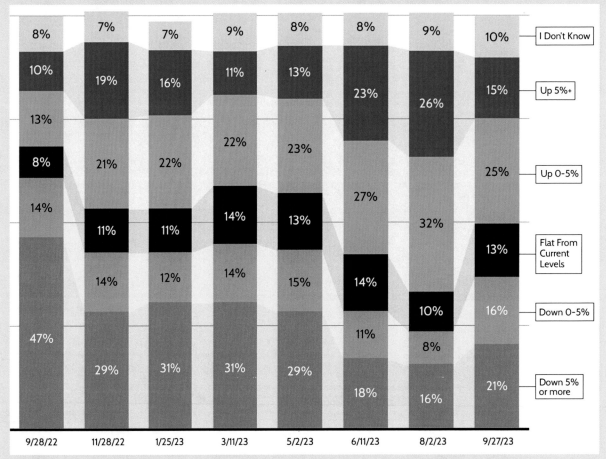

Dates reflect end of fielding period. N>740 invested readers per date.
Source: Investopedia Reader Survey, 18+ U.S.

UNDERSTANDING INDEX FUNDS

Since the first index fund—the Vanguard 500—debuted in 1976, index funds have become a popular form of passive stock market investing. An index fund is a type of mutual fund or ETF designed to track and follow the performance of a specific financial market index, or a group of companies represented on a stock exchange.

Mutual funds are run by fund managers who oversee which businesses are included in the funds at any given time; fund managers charge a fee for their research and time. ETFs are computer-generated funds that trade like stocks, so they can be bought and sold at any time during the day. Index funds are also computer generated, but they can only be bought or sold according to the price at the end of the day.

Index funds save investors money over time simply because they have lower fees than human-managed mutual funds.

Sheinbein says that, over time, most investments do not outperform the S&P 500. He suggests investors should ask themselves, "Why would I pay a larger fee for something that underperforms the thing it is benchmarked against?"

In contrast, index funds have very low fees (Vanguard index funds can be as low as 0.03%), whereas the average mutual fund charges anywhere from 0.6% to 1.2%, he says.

This fee difference can mean significant savings for an investor as the portfolio grows and interest compounds year on year.

Financial planner Lanesha Mohip, MBA, MHRM, adds that index funds are a great option for people looking to invest their money in something low-cost, low-expense, diversified, and long-term. They are generally considered ideal portfolio holdings for retirement accounts such as 401(k)s or individual retirement accounts (IRAs), which have a long time to mature. But there are many index funds to choose from, and that's where investors might get tripped up.

"Each investment strategy has a different goal . . . you have to have an end goal," Mohip says. "Some of us may have long-term asset appreciation goals, so it wouldn't make any sense for me to invest in small companies that are growing— that have no skin in the game right now. I need to invest in large-capitalization companies that have proven they've earned billions of dollars," she says.

Investors with these goals might want an index fund that includes Apple, Visa, and John Deere, for example. But if the goal is to invest in aggressive companies that are innovative in their niche, then maybe the Russell 2000 index is a better mix of companies.

The index fund that's right for you, Mohip adds, depends on your goal: short-term cash flow, long-term appreciation, growing a portfolio. "Every one of these has a different purpose," she says.

There are index funds for nearly every segment of the market. Some well-known indexes include:
• The S&P 500 index: represents the

roughly 500 leading U.S. large-capitalization companies
• The Dow Jones Industrial Average (DJIA): represents 30 large-cap U.S. companies
• The Nasdaq Composite index (COMP): comprised of approximately 3,000 NASDAQ-listed stocks, mostly from the technology sector
• The Russell 2000 index: represents 2,000 small-capitalization U.S. stocks

INDEX FUNDS AND YOUR PORTFOLIO

Aside from low costs, index funds are generally considered lower-risk than both individual stocks and actively managed funds. However, they are not entirely risk-free.

Since they follow a specific index, market fluctuations, economic shifts, and changes in interest rates can impact an index fund's performance.

Every fund is exposed to a wide range of stocks or bonds within that index. This diversification spreads the risk and reduces the impact of potentially poor-performing individual securities.

To balance a portfolio of riskier investments, index funds provide broad market exposure and save investors on fees.

HOW TO INVEST IN INDEX FUNDS

Evaluate Your Portfolio
In order to choose the right index fund for you, you first need to evaluate your current investments— i.e., retirement accounts, real estate, bonds, and stocks—to see how index funds can be added to reach your goals.

Index funds can be bought through a brokerage account or an index-fund provider. Many different companies, such as Vanguard or Fidelity, offer

WARNING

Owning an index fund does not mean you are immune from risk or losses if the markets take a downturn.

MORE ABOUT MARKET CAP

SMALL-CAP
A company with a total market value, or market capitalization, of $250 million to $2 billion. Small-cap stocks have historically outperformed large-cap stocks but are more volatile and riskier.

MID-CAP
A company with a market value generally between $2 billion and $10 billion. Mid-cap companies are usually in the middle of their growth curve and are expected to post sustained increases in their profits, market share, and productivity.

LARGE-CAP
Also called big-cap, this is a company with a market capitalization value of more than $10 billion. Large-cap stocks represent a significant portion of the U.S. equity market and are often used as core portfolio holdings.

competitively priced and well-performing index funds.

Instead of having several accounts at different brokerages, Mohip recommends seeing whether your existing bank or employer is already in business with a brokerage company. "The more assets you have in one brokerage, the lower your investment fee, or your overall fee to do business with them," she says.

Do Your Research
Next, it's time for index-level research. Since index funds include hundreds of companies—as opposed to stocks that you can handpick—you'll want to understand the brokerage company's fact sheet, its prospectus, and the range of index fund options it offers.

This is particularly important for investors who want to balance their financial goals with ethical ones. For example, environmental, social, and governance (ESG)–focused index funds consider more than just returns.

These funds might include companies with diverse leadership teams, a climate risk mitigation platform, and a strong history of corporate social responsibility efforts. These kinds of index funds are well-researched by the brokerage before they are launched, and this unique grouping of companies may only be found at one brokerage and not another.

Open a Brokerage Account
Once you've done your research, you can open a brokerage account, fund the particular index(es) you've selected, and monitor the portfolio over time. Mohip suggests checking in at least annually to see if you're still on track. This doesn't mean just checking the rate of return on the index fund; it means checking in on

that foundational budget, based on living expenses and high-interest debt balances.

"There's a level of discipline that's needed for consistency in investing, but also, life happens," she says. "We have children, we get partners, we lose partners, we build businesses, we have parents to take care of. Life happens in the span of 12 months, so you want to have eyeballs on all of your money. I don't care if it's short-term money or long-term money."

APPLYING THE RULES
When it comes to applying the Investopedia investing rules, there are three to consider for index funds specifically:

Start Now!
Time is on your side when it comes to investing, and index funds are typically long-term investments. Thanks to the compounding effect, the more time allotted for the investment to mature, the greater the return is likely to be down the line.

Sheinbein recommends investing early and consistently to reap the benefits of compounding returns. "If you invest continuously over time and you have time on your side, the compound effect will be huge," he says.

Aim for Balance
Diversification is one of the key benefits of investing in index funds. Buying shares of an index fund exposes you to all the stocks in an index, adding balance to your portfolio without requiring you to invest in hundreds or thousands of individual stocks.

You could also invest in multiple index funds focused on particular sectors, which helps add balance to your portfolio by spreading your

S&P 500 Index Offers 9.77% 10-Year Returns

Despite short-term fluctuations, the historical performance of S&P Dow Jones Indices (SPX) shows long-term growth.

> Oct. 16, 2023
> $4,373.63

Source: S&P Dow Jones Indices

investment across more than one sector, such as energy, technology, or consumer goods. When one sector underperforms, a different sector might help to lift your portfolio.

Be a Tax-Efficient Investor
Index funds are "naturally tax-efficient," according to the investment firm Vanguard, meaning they result in lower taxes for investors. That's because index funds mimic the composition of a financial market index, and they buy and sell stocks less frequently, minimizing short-term capital gains, which are subject to higher taxes.

Index funds also result in fewer fees and commissions than actively managed funds.

THE BOTTOM LINE

Offering market diversification and lower fees, index funds are a valuable component of any investment portfolio. It's important to consider your financial goals, risk tolerance, and investment timeline before deciding which index fund is right for you. Also, while they are considered passive investing, index funds can still be vulnerable to market fluctuations and crashes. ⓔ

SCAN HERE

Check out Investopedia's recommendations for the Best Brokers for Beginners to support your investing journey.

STOCKS ETFS BONDS INDEX FUNDS

Investing Outside the Box: Alternative Assets

Know the risks, tax rates, and viability before you dive in

The term alternative investment simply refers to an investment being an alternative to stocks and bonds. Both an unboxed Star Wars figurine with appreciating value and a run-down local warehouse could fall into the definition of an alternative investment.

Common forms of alternative investments include private equity or venture capital, cryptocurrency, hedge funds, managed futures, art and antiques, commodities, and derivatives contracts. Real estate is also often classified as an alternative investment.

Most alternative investments are subject to fewer regulations from the U.S. Securities and Exchange Commission (SEC) and tend to be somewhat illiquid, meaning they are not easily sold and converted to cash.

That said, alternative investments can help keep your portfolio balanced if leveraged carefully. Here's what you should know.

UNDERSTANDING ALTERNATIVE INVESTMENTS

Many alternative investment assets are held by institutional investors or accredited high-net-worth individuals because of their complex nature, lack of regulation, and degree of risk.

Many alternative investments also have high minimum investments and fee structures, especially when compared with mutual funds and exchange-traded funds (ETFs). These investments also have less opportunity to publish verifiable performance data and advertise to potential investors.

Although alternative assets may have high initial minimums and up-front investment fees, the transaction costs are typically lower than those of conventional assets due to lower levels of turnover.

Most alternative assets are fairly illiquid, especially compared to their conventional counterparts.

For example, investors are likely to find it considerably more difficult to sell an 80-year old bottle of wine than 1,000 shares of Apple, due to a limited number of potential buyers.

Investors may have difficulty even valuing alternative investments, since the assets and transactions involving them are often rare. For example, a seller of a 1933 Saint-Gaudens Double Eagle $20 gold coin may have difficulty determining its value, as there are only 11 known to exist but only one that can be owned by an individual, legally.

TYPES OF ALTERNATIVE INVESTMENTS

Real Estate

Real estate as an investment includes investing in physical properties or property-based securities such as real estate investment trusts (REITs), real estate mutual funds, or crowdfunding platforms. In addition to capital appreciation of tangible assets, real estate investors strive for operating income to potentially provide ongoing stable cash flow.

MORE ON P. 68

Commodities

Commodities are raw materials such as gold, silver, oil, and agricultural products. Investors can invest in these tangible goods that have real-world uses and often perpetual demand due to the underlying characteristics of what they are. For example, gold's price is arguably more stable because it's used in a variety of industries.

Art and Collectibles

Some investments may double as a hobby, with art, sports memorabilia, entertainment memorabilia, or other collectibles acting as alternative investments. These items may have historical worth or develop worth over time as related parties (i.e., the artist, associated movie star, or associated athlete) become more historic.

Cryptocurrencies

Cryptocurrencies such as Bitcoin, Tether, and Ethereum surged in popularity over the past few years, but they are still considered alternative assets and are largely unregulated in the U.S. Though some may claim cryptocurrency does not offer a strong hedge against other risk-on investments, it may provide capital appreciation or passive income due to staking rewards.

Venture Capital/Private Equity

Blurring the lines of an alternative investment, venture capital or private equity are simply a refined branch of stock investments. Instead of trading shares of public companies in an open market, investors may seek alternative avenues to put capital into private companies or startups.

MORE ON P. 70

REGULATIONS

Even when they don't involve unique items such as coins or art, alternative investments are vulnerable to investment scams and fraud due to the lack of regulations.

Alternative investments are often subject to a less-clear legal structure than conventional investments. They do fall under the purview of the Dodd-Frank Wall Street Reform and Consumer Protection Act, and their practices are subject to examination by the SEC.

However, they usually don't have to register with the SEC. As such, they are not overseen or regulated by the SEC the way mutual funds and ETFs are. So it is essential that investors conduct extensive due diligence when they are considering investing in alternative assets.

HOW TO INVEST

Getting started with investing in alternative investments is very different based on the alternative you're working with. Some may require substantial capital and research; others may simply require a few clicks of a mouse button. Here are some examples.

Commodities

Commodity investments involve buying physical assets such as gold, silver, oil, or agricultural products. Investors can also participate in commodity investments through commodity trading platforms, exchange-traded funds (ETFs), or mutual funds.

Art and Collectibles

Investors can invest in art and collectibles through art dealers, auction houses, or online marketplaces. Due to the uniqueness of these goods, consider the reputation of the dealer when exploring avenues to trade.

Cryptocurrencies

Investors can invest in cryptocurrencies though cryptocurrency exchanges, brokers, or online platforms. Investors must often deposit domestic currency into a digital wallet that will house the private keys and currencies of that investor.

TAX IMPLICATIONS

Because they represent an entirely different asset class than stocks and bonds, many alternative investments have different tax rules.

In addition, consider how different alternatives may have different income streams (i.e., capital gain on the sale of a rental property in addition to rent revenue).

Some alternative investments such as collectibles and art may not offer the same tax deductions as traditional investments such as stocks and bonds.

WARNING

Most alternative investments incur a transaction or processing fee, so be mindful of maintenance or one-time fees when investing.

Pros and Cons of Alternative Investments

PROS	CONS
✓ May offer diversification benefits	✗ Are often associated with higher fees and transaction costs
✓ Often have higher return potential than traditional investments	✗ Often have higher risk than traditional investments
✓ May offer protection against inflation	✗ Often lack regulation or transparency
✓ May allow investors to more specifically select investment preferences	✗ May be more volatile than traditional investments
✓ May be illiquid and more difficult to panic sell, creating unofficial price and value protection	✗ May be illiquid and more difficult to sell, creating barriers for those trying to liquidate

In addition, collectibles such as art or coins are explicitly defined by the IRS as a collectible, and net capital gains on them are subject to a maximum 28% tax rate.

Cryptocurrency and other digital asset tax rules continue to evolve. Digital assets such as virtual currency, cryptocurrency, stablecoins, and non-fungible tokens may incur taxable transactions when selling the asset for fiat, exchanging the asset for goods or services, or exchanging the asset for another digital asset.

In addition, whereas fluctuations in the value of the U.S. dollar would not incur a taxable event, fluctuations in value of digital assets often result in capital gains or losses.

Some alternative investments such as real estate and certain types of energy investments may offer tax-deferred or tax-free investing options.

This may include 1031 Exchanges and Opportunity Zone investments, where investors can use proceeds from the sale of an alternative asset to invest in a similar or specific asset to avoid taxes.

APPLYING THE RULES

Tame Your Animal Spirits

Alternative investments can involve a great deal of risk. Consider what level of risk you're comfortable with, and don't let emotions like fear or greed drive your investing decisions.

Instead of acting on impulse or following the herd, take time to consider whether a certain investment is right for you. Do your research, and be mindful of the psychological traps, such as overconfidence and confirmation bias, that can interfere with sound investment decisions.

Better Safe Than Sorry

Don't make alternative investments just because you see friends, celebrities, or social media influencers making those investments.

It's easy to get swept up in certain trends—the hype around cryptocurrency or non-fungible tokens (NFTs), for example—but every investor should do their research and make careful decisions that align with their risk tolerance and financial goals. Think twice before you borrow money or tap your retirement account just to be able to buy a Bored Ape NFT. If that investment goes south, it's your own financial future on the line.

Aim for Balance

Alternative investments can help add balance to your portfolio. But as with any investment, don't put all your eggs in one basket, and don't put your entire portfolio into riskier alternative assets. Instead, alternative assets can be one part of a balanced portfolio that also includes stocks and bonds.

Alternative investments—from fine art to gold to private equity—are typically not tied to stock market performance, so they can add diversification that helps your portfolio withstand a market downturn.

THE BOTTOM LINE

As you embark on your alternative investment journey, consider speaking with a financial advisor in addition to a tax advisor to best understand how to protect your assets and ensure maximum efficiency in protecting your returns. ❷

| STOCKS | ETFS | BONDS | INDEX FUNDS |

Unlocking Property Wealth

Dos and don'ts for aspiring real estate investors

BY NATHAN REIFF

Real estate is an asset class that retail investors often overlook, but it can hold an important place in a balanced and diversified portfolio. One reason for the underutilization of real estate investments is that many investors believe these products to be out of reach, except for those holding significant capital.

Fortunately, there are a variety of ways to gain exposure to real estate, even for those who are only able to invest a modest amount.

WAYS TO INVEST

Rental Properties
Residential properties such as apartments, townhouses, and standalone homes can be rented out for additional income (although investors should be aware of expenses and responsibilities associated with becoming a landlord). Properties rented out through short-term homestay companies such as Airbnb and Vrbo may be included in this list.

House Flipping
For those with significant experience navigating the market and both capital and time to dedicate to the endeavor, buying properties and renovating or developing new homes can be lucrative.

Online Real Estate Platforms
Individuals may find it easiest to focus on real estate investments by pooling money with like-minded investors through an online real estate platform or real estate crowdfunding platform like RealtyMogul or Yieldstreet. However, these investments may be illiquid and include management fees.

REITs
A real estate investment trust (REIT) pools investor money to buy and operate income-generating real estate. Investors can broaden their portfolios to include this asset class while not needing to participate in traditional real estate transactions. Benefits of REITs include a requirement to pay out regular dividends of at least 90% of taxable income each year, as well as the ease of trading like stocks on major exchanges. Investors considering REITs,

crowdfunded investing, and similar approaches can gain access to real estate assets without having to put up a massive amount of capital.

REIGs

Real estate investment groups (REIGs) are set up like small mutual funds. Investors dedicate capital to a shared investment in rental properties, such as a group of apartments or condos. Individual investors can buy properties from within the group of units in order to rent them out. REIGs can help mitigate risk and reduce or even eliminate many of the burdens of owning and operating a rental property.

PROS

Tax Benefits

Rental property income is not taxed as self-employment income, and real estate investors may be eligible for certain government benefits, such as lower tax rates on profits over the long term.

Cash Flow Potential

Buying residential and commercial properties requires significant capital up front, but these investments can provide substantial and steady cash flow following the initial investment. Luis Rosa, CFP, creator of the "On My Way to Wealth" podcast, says that properties with "positive cash flow … may be a great long-term investment."

Appreciation

Real estate investments often appreciate over time, particularly if you, as owner, keep up with maintenance and upgrades.

More Accessible Options

Investors considering REITs, crowdfunded investing, and similar approaches can gain access to real estate assets without having to put up a massive amount of capital.

CONS

Heightened Risk Potential

The market exposes investors—and, in particular, first-time real estate investors—to a much higher level of risk than most other asset classes.

Melanie Fleet, a Massachusetts-based Realtor, cautions that "if it looks too good to be true, it often is," adding that investing in real estate is "not as easy as it might look."

Doing your research and having a good team to help you is crucial. Fleet says such a team might include accountants, real estate agents, property managers, and others.

Liabilities & Responsibilities

Owning rental property or real estate to flip and sell may expose an investor to liabilities—for example, if individuals on the property are injured. Thomas Catalano, president of Hilton Head Wealth Advisors, cautions investors who are not handy or otherwise comfortable with the ins and outs of property upkeep, eviction laws, and related areas to "walk before they run."

Overleveraging

Real estate investments may come with substantial additional costs beyond the property. Taxes, upkeep, and the cost of finding and screening tenants are among the many variables.

Dividend Taxes

Investors should beware of taxes associated with dividends paid out by REITs, as well as other fees that may be unique to investing in real estate and related funds.

APPLYING THE RULES

Time Is Everything

Most real estate professionals agree: There's no sense in trying to time the market. A host of factors contribute to real estate prices, including local and national demand, materials costs, trends in population shifts and changes in work habits, the Federal Reserve's approach to interest rates, the health of banks, and the status of the broader economy, among others. These variables mean trying to find the bottom of the market is, in most cases, a fruitless endeavor.

But timing is still important. For investors looking at buying properties, it's key to keep track of Fed rate movements, which often impact lender mortgage rates.

Better Safe Than Sorry

For most investors, buying or selling a property such as a house or apartment is the largest single transaction of their lifetime. When buying real estate, it's essential not to overinvest, make excessively risky borrowing decisions, or concentrate your investment too heavily.

THE BOTTOM LINE

A common misconception is that you need massive amounts of capital to invest in real estate. In reality, REITs, pooled funds, and other innovative strategies provide different access points, but real estate investments are not to be taken lightly. They're often complicated and may involve hidden costs and risks. REITs tend to be associated with the lowest level of risk and the smallest workload for investors, making them a good entry point.

Investors able to manage these concerns can enjoy the likelihood of appreciating assets, a steady income stream, tax benefits, and more. ✷

STOCKS — ETFS — BONDS — INDEX FUNDS

Are Private Equity Investments Right for You?

BY ADAM HAYES

You might think private equity is a playground exclusively for the super-rich or Wall Street insiders. But there are more accessible ways for everyday investors to get exposure to private companies and startups, potentially boosting returns.

Here's what you need to know about private equity.

PRIVATE EQUITY 101
- Venture capital (VC)—provides funding for brand new startups and early-stage businesses.
- Growth capital (mezzanine financing)—invests in more mature

private firms looking to expand.
- Leveraged buyouts (LBOs)—allow investment firms to acquire businesses using debt.

Private equity can offer exposure to young companies with more growth potential than you can get from public stocks. Investors can also target specific sectors, such as tech or healthcare.

For example, private equity has funded many well-known startups in recent years, including Airbnb, Pinterest, and Uber before they went public. Some well-known companies like Publix Supermarkets and SpaceX are still only available via private investment.

Be aware that there is some survivorship bias going on, in that we only hear about the small handful of unicorns or other successful startups that have made it big.

What you don't often hear about are the numerous startups or other privately held firms that didn't succeed—the ones that fizzled out, went bankrupt, or just never took off.

So while the potential for high returns is tempting, it's crucial to remember that the risks are equally high. Always do your due diligence and consult with financial advisors to be sure you're making informed decisions.

Another note: Because private equity involves putting money into companies that aren't publicly traded, they don't have to follow as many rules and regulations about sharing information. This makes it harder to know what you're really investing in, and the risk of losing money is therefore higher.

Because of these risks, the government has rules that say only accredited investors—those who are considered experienced or financially stable enough to handle the risk—can get involved.

HOW TO INVEST

A private equity fund is managed by a private equity firm. To invest you must be an accredited investor or a qualified client. Often these are institutional investors such as insurance companies, university endowments, and pension funds.

According to the U.S. Securities and Exchange Commission, to be an accredited investor, you must earn an income in excess of $200,000 (and have for the last two years.), have a net worth over $1 million, or hold in good standing a Series 7, 65, or 82 license.

If you qualify and are interested in private equity, research the largest private equity firms such as Blackstone, KKR, EQT, and The Carlyle Group. Alternatively, you can seek exposure to private equity investments through investing in publicly traded private equity firms like Blackstone and KKR, or consider a private equity filled ETF such as the Invesco Global Listed Private Equity Portfolio or ProShares Global Listed Private Equity Portfolio.

THE PROS AND CONS

Private equity provides several benefits for investors beyond public market exposure:

- Potential for higher returns compared with public stocks and bonds
- More direct involvement in helping the company grow and succeed
- Low correlation to other asset classes

There are also risks, which include:

- Illiquidity—it's not easy to cash out investments quickly
- Higher fees than traditional investments, which can eat into returns
- Less transparency and regulation than investing in public companies

Because of its unique risks and lower transparency, private equity is best suited for more sophisticated investors who have a long time horizon of 10-plus years and can withstand volatility.

Zaneilia Harris, CFP, president of Harris & Harris Wealth Management Group in Upper Marlboro, Md., cautions, "Investors need to have a clear understanding of what the investment is before they put their money into an alternative asset class like private equity. Don't be sold the investment—instead, determine for yourself [along with the help of your advisor] if it is appropriate and a reasonable risk."

A small portfolio allocation of less than 10% is recommended for most individual investors. It should be viewed as an alternative asset to complement stocks and bonds, not replace them entirely.

APPLYING THE RULES

Be a Tax-Efficient Investor

Accessing private equity through a fund versus a direct investment can make a big difference in capital gains tax exposure. When you invest through a fund or ETF, you're typically subject to the fund's own tax structure, which might distribute gains in a way that could be taxed at a higher rate.

On the other hand, direct investments in private equity often qualify for long-term capital gains tax rates, which are generally lower than short-term rates, provided you hold the investment for over a year. Always consult a tax advisor to understand the nuances of your specific situation and to plan accordingly.

Manage Your Risk

Private equity is riskier than most public market investments, given its lower liquidity and transparency. Only invest money you won't need access to for the long-term and are prepared to lose.

THE BOTTOM LINE

Private equity can enhance portfolio returns and diversification for suitable investors. Focus on funds for easier access, start small, and do your due diligence on any investment, and partner with trusted managers. Used selectively, private equity can boost your overall investing strategy. ❷

STOCKS — ETFS — BONDS — INDEX FUNDS

Navigating the High-Stakes World of Hedge Funds

Strategies, risks, and regulations explained

BY ADAM HAYES

Y ou've probably heard about hedge funds—those elusive investment pools seemingly reserved for the ultra-rich., like what's depicted in the Showtime TV series *Billions*. But what if you, an everyday investor, could also get a slice of the hedge fund pie?

While many do remain exclusive, hedge funds are no longer the territory of only Wall Street insiders and billionaire investors. Thanks to changes in regulations and investment platforms, these doors are slowly opening for more people to participate.

Here, you'll learn the basics of what hedge funds are, the different types available, and what you should consider before taking the plunge.

UNPACKING HEDGE FUNDS

Hedge funds pool money from various investors to buy a variety of assets.

Unlike mutual funds, hedge funds aim for higher returns and are less constrained by regulation, which allows them the flexibility to engage in more complex strategies, like short selling and the use of derivatives and leverage.

Managed by professionals, hedge funds aim to beat the market and earn excess returns.

Hedge funds employ a range of strategies, from betting on the rise or fall of stocks to investing in real estate or commodities. However, the promise of higher returns also comes with higher fees and greater risks.

In terms of regulation, hedge funds are subject to fewer rules than other investments, but they are still overseen by regulatory bodies such as the Securities and Exchange Commission (SEC) in the United States.

Historically, hedge funds were the domain of "accredited investors"—a regulatory term for individuals who have a net worth exceeding $1 million (excluding their primary residence) or an annual income of $200,000 or more.

However, recent changes have started to make hedge funds more accessible to the average investor.

Some funds have lowered their minimum investment requirements, and certain platforms now offer "hedge fund–like" products that replicate hedge fund strategies but are available to retail investors in the form of exchange-traded funds (ETFs).

These alternatives offer lower-net-worth investors access to part of the hedge fund world. However, they still come with unique risks and cost structures that warrant careful evaluation.

TYPES OF HEDGE FUNDS

Hedge funds come in various flavors, each with its own investment focus and risk profile. Below are some of the most common types of hedge funds, detailed to give you a clearer idea of what each entails.

Long/Short Equity Funds

These funds take both long and short positions in stocks. The goal is to profit from both rising and falling markets, thereby hedging against market volatility.

Global Macro Hedge Funds

These funds place bets on macroeconomic conditions and trends, such as interest rates, currency movements, and economic policies. They're typically less concerned with individual companies and focused on broader economic themes.

Trend-Following Hedge Funds

Also known as Commodity Trading Advisors (CTA), these use statistical models to identify trends in various asset classes like stocks, bonds, currencies, and commodities.

Relative Value Hedge Funds

These funds aim to exploit price discrepancies between related financial instruments. For example, they might buy a corporate bond while simultaneously selling a different bond from the same issuer, betting that the price gap between the two will narrow or widen.

Activist Hedge Funds

These funds take substantial equity positions in companies and then use that influence to push for changes such as restructuring or management shifts with the aim of increasing shareholder value.

They often engage directly with company boards and may even seek seats to effect their desired changes.

Quantitative Funds

Managed by data scientists, or "quants," these funds use complex algorithms and models to identify trading opportunities, often at a very high frequency.

Event-Driven Funds

These focus on specific events such as mergers, acquisitions, or bankruptcies that could trigger stock price changes.

WHAT TO CONSIDER

Hedge funds are not one-size-fits-all investments. They often require a substantial minimum investment—sometimes in the millions—and therefore, many remain suitable only for accredited investors.

They can also charge hefty fees, often a management fee plus a percentage of profits. They're less transparent and less liquid than other investments, making them harder to value.

Generally, they're suited for higher-net-worth individuals who can stomach the risk, afford the minimum investment, and handle having their money locked up for a period of some years.

THE BOTTOM LINE

Hedge funds offer the allure of high returns and sophisticated investment strategies, but they're not for everyone. They operate in a less regulated environment, employ complex tactics, and often come with high fees and minimum investment requirements.

Ideal for high-net-worth individuals willing to take on more risk, hedge funds may be an intriguing option—but they require careful consideration to determine if this exclusive investment avenue aligns with your objectives. ❧

Delta, Theta, Gamma, What?

Before you trade options, make sure you understand the Greeks

Trading derivatives, including options, is a next-level investing strategy that should be explored with caution, and only after you've learned all about a collection of risk-assessment variables referred to as "the Greeks." Here's why:

Options are financial derivatives, which are securities with underlying assets (such as stocks or indexes) that dictate pricing, risk, and basic term structure. Traders use options to speculate on the direction of price, to hedge or reduce the risk of their portfolios, and make contract decisions informed by the Greeks.

WHAT ARE THE GREEKS?
A Greek symbol is used to designate each risk variable, namely delta, theta, gamma, vega, and rho. Each Greek has a number value that provides information about how the option is moving or the risk associated with buying or selling that option.

These values change over time, so savvy traders will check them daily or multiple times a day before making trades to assess risk, manage their option portfolio, or check whether their portfolio needs to be balanced.

Δ Delta
Delta represents the rate of change between the option's price and a $1 change in the underlying asset's price. In other words, the price sensitivity of the option is relative to the underlying asset.

The delta also tells options traders the hedging ratio to become delta neutral. A third interpretation of an option's delta is the probability that it will finish in the money. Delta values can be positive or negative depending on the type of option.

Θ Theta
Theta represents the rate of change between the option price and time, or time sensitivity, sometimes known as an option's time decay. Time decay means an option loses value as time moves closer to its maturity, as long as everything is held constant.

The measure of theta quantifies the risk that time poses to option buyers, since options are only exercisable for a certain period of time.

Theta is generally expressed as a negative number for long positions and as a positive number for short positions. It can be thought of as the amount by which an option's value declines every day.

Γ Gamma
Gamma represents the rate of change between an option's delta and the underlying asset's price. This is called second-order (second-derivative) price sensitivity. Gamma indicates the amount the delta would change given a $1 move in the underlying security.

Gamma is used to determine how stable an option's delta is: The higher the gamma, the more volatile the price of the option is.

Options traders may opt to not only hedge delta but also gamma in order to be delta-gamma neutral, meaning that as the underlying price moves, the delta will remain close to zero.

ν Vega
Vega is a derivative of implied volatility and lets option traders know how much the price of the option could swing based on changes in the underlying asset.

Volatility measures the amount and speed at which price moves up and down and can be based on recent changes in price, historical price changes, and expected price moves in a trading instrument.

Vega rises as the option gets closer to the strike price at-the-money. Vega falls as the option moves away from the strike price either in-the-money or out-of-the-money. Future-dated options have positive vega while options that are expiring immediately have negative vega.

ρ Rho
Rho measures the price change for a derivative relative to a change in the risk-free rate of interest. Rho may

also refer to the aggregated risk exposure to interest rate changes that exist for a book of several options positions.

IMPLIED AND HISTORIC VOLATILITY

Implied volatility is not a Greek, but it is related. This theoretical value forecasts how volatile the stock underlying an option will be in the future. It shows what is expected, but it is not always dependable.

Implied volatility is usually reflected in the price of an option and can help traders judge what assumptions market makers are using to set their bid and ask prices, such as:
· Upcoming earnings reports
· Pending product launches
· Expected mergers or acquisitions

Historic volatility (HV) measures the range of returns of an index or security over a specific time period. If an asset's historical volatility is going up, that means its price is moving further away from its average (in either direction) faster than usual.

Comparing an underlying stock's historic volatility with its implied volatility can help you judge whether the option you are considering is priced low or high. If the implied volatility is higher than normal, this generally benefits option sellers. Implied volatility that is lower than normal, usually benefits option buyers.

THE BOTTOM LINE

Market conditions are constantly changing, and the Greeks help determine how sensitive a specific trade is to price fluctuations, volatility, and the passage of time. It's not enough to just know the total capital at risk in an options position. To understand the probability of a trade making money, you must be able to determine a variety of risk-exposure measurements. ℤ

SCAN HERE

Interested in options trading?
Read our full guide
before you get started.

A Closer Look

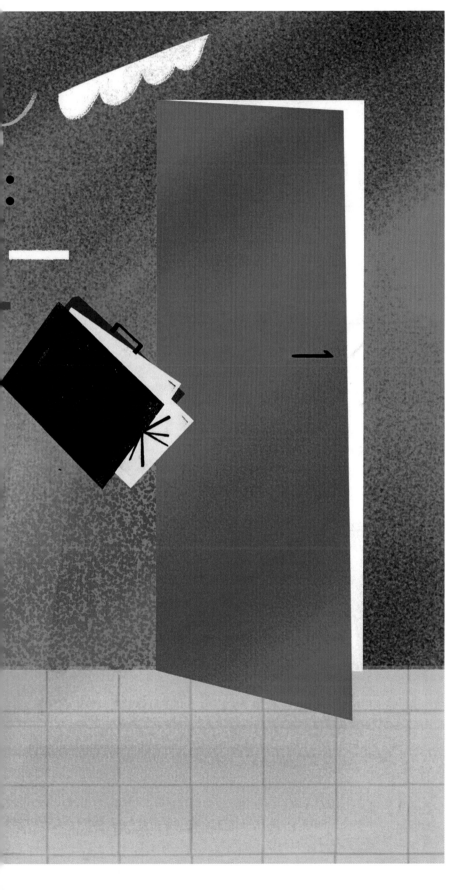

How Strategy Can Change Your Portfolio

And how to apply the rules when it does

Your investment strategy refers to a set of principles designed to help an individual investor achieve their financial and investment goals. As you learned from the quiz in this book, investors can follow different strategies, varying from conservative to aggressive, depending on who they are and their financial situation.

As you get older and your lifestyle and goals change, so will the choices and decisions you make as an investor. Here, we dive deeper into how strategy can impact your portfolio.

WHAT TO FACTOR IN
Investment strategies are styles of investing that help individuals meet their short- and long-term goals. Strategies depend on a variety of factors, including:
• Age
• Goals
• Where you live
• Lifestyle
• Financial situation

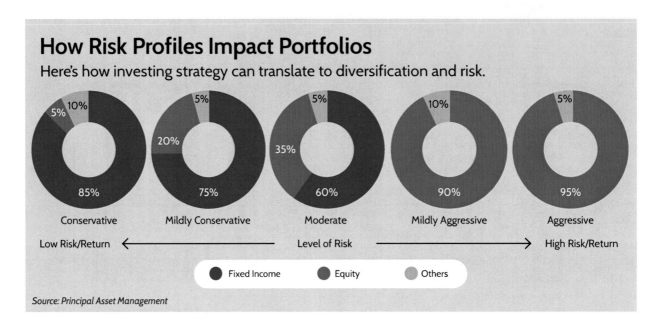

How Risk Profiles Impact Portfolios
Here's how investing strategy can translate to diversification and risk.

Conservative — 5%, 10%, 85%
Mildly Conservative — 5%, 20%, 75%
Moderate — 5%, 35%, 60%
Mildly Aggressive — 10%, 90%
Aggressive — 5%, 95%

Low Risk/Return ← Level of Risk → High Risk/Return

● Fixed Income   ● Equity   ● Others

Source: Principal Asset Management

IMPORTANT
—
Because investment strategies depend so heavily on your personal situation and goals, it's important to do your research before you commit your capital to any investment.

• Available capital
• Expected returns

The above isn't an exhaustive list, of course. Yours may include other details that are specific to you as an individual investor. These factors help an investor determine the kind of investments they want to purchase, including stocks, bonds, money market funds, and real estate; asset allocation; and how much risk they can tolerate.

For example, a 25-year-old who is new to their career and has no dependents may consider riskier investments such as stocks and real estate, because they have more time to invest and are more tolerant to risk. In the event the market takes a dive, they can afford to lose some money, as they have time on their side—one of the most powerful tools in an investor's toolbox.

A 45-year-old, on the other hand, does not have as much time for compounding to kick in and therefore would be better off with a more conservative plan that ensures they will be financially secure in retirement. They may consider investing in things such as bonds, government securities, and other safer bets.

KNOW YOUR RISK TOLERANCE
Risk is a huge component of an investment strategy. Some individuals have a high tolerance for risk, while other investors are risk-averse.

People who are more open to risk, or who have a longer investment horizon, tend to employ aggressive plans because they have a longer timeline, while those who want to preserve capital are more likely to take a conservative approach. It comes down to personal preference, too. As noted, investment strategies range from conservative plans to highly aggressive ones. Here, we dive into each strategy a bit deeper.

Conservative
Conservative investing is a strategy that prioritizes the preservation of capital over growth or market returns. This type of investment plan employs safe investments that generally come with low risks and provide stable returns. It's typically used by those who have a low tolerance for risk.

Usually, a conservative investment strategy will include a relatively high weighting to low-risk securities, such as Treasuries (government bonds) and other high-quality bonds, money markets, and cash equivalents.

Many conservative investors buy low-cost, diversified index funds, use dollar-cost averaging, and reinvest their dividends. Dollar-cost averaging is an investment strategy where a fixed dollar amount of stocks or a particular investment are acquired on a regular schedule regardless of the cost of the investment or the share price.

Aggressive

If you think of investment strategies on a scale, aggressive would be on the opposite end of conservative. Highly aggressive strategies are those that involve risky investments such as stocks, options, and junk bonds, with the goal of generating maximum returns. Young adults with smaller portfolios are more likely to lean in this direction due to their lengthy investment horizon and high risk tolerance. No matter one's age, though, having a high risk tolerance is essential for those taking on an aggressive strategy.

Aggressive strategies typically require more hands-on active management rather than a buy-and-hold strategy. Because of this, it is usually best for more experienced investors who will select individual stocks and build a portfolio based on individual firm analysis with predictions on share price movements.

Balanced (Moderate)

A balanced portfolio is generally utilized by someone who falls somewhere in the middle of aggressive and conservative. This strategy prioritizes both capital preservation and growth, rather than just one of those things.

Typically, balanced portfolios are divided between stocks and bonds, either equally or with a slight tilt, such as 60% to 40%. In some cases, this type of portfolio also includes a small cash or money market component for liquidity purposes.

VALUE INVESTING VS. GROWTH INVESTING

Some investors may choose strategies such as value and growth investing.

With value investing, an investor chooses stocks that look as though they trade for less than their intrinsic value. This type of investor believes the market overreacts to good and bad news, resulting in stock price movements that generally do not correspond to a company's long-term fundamentals. With this opportunity, the investor purchases the stock at a discounted price.

Growth investing, on the other hand, is more focused on increasing an investor's capital. With this strategy, individuals invest in young or small companies whose earnings are expected to increase at an above-average rate compared with their industry sector or the overall market. While this strategy can be highly lucrative, it's also fairly high-risk, as these companies are often untried.

THE BOTTOM LINE

An investment strategy is a plan designed to help an individual investor achieve their financial and investment goals. When choosing from a conservative, moderate, or aggressive strategy, you should think about your age, capital, risk tolerance, and goals. As your personal situation changes, you should reevaluate your investment strategy and readjust accordingly.

Depending on their experience and knowledge, people can choose to make investment decisions on their own or by working with a financial professional. Keep in mind that there is no right way to manage a portfolio, but investors should always do their own research, using facts and data to back up their decisions, ultimately keeping risk low and maintaining sufficient liquidity. ⊘

4 Strategy Tips

1. WRITE IT DOWN

Once you have an idea of what strategy you want to adopt, write down your process and how you're going to get there. Whether it's on a computer or with pen and paper, make sure you can access it easily.

2. BELIEVE IN YOUR PLAN

For a plan to truly be successful, you have to want to follow through with it and believe in it. Your unique knowledge, through research and experience, is your competitive advantage. Use it regularly.

3. MAKE IT RESILIENT

Good investment managers know where performance comes from and can explain not only their strategy's strengths but also its weaknesses. This will allow you to maintain confidence, invest with conviction, and find alternative moves that complement your own.

4. MEASURE IT

Having a benchmark to measure the effectiveness of your strategy will help you learn, improve, and better understand the process. Your benchmark should match your financial goals, which should match your strategy. Do this by setting a target return percentage or comparing your results with a passive market index, such as the S&P 500.

The Impact of Behavioral Investing on Your Portfolio

How to recognize and overcome your financial biases

BY ERIN GOBLER

Money is an inherently emotional topic. Everything from the large-scale financial events happening in the world around us to the way money comes and goes from our own bank accounts and portfolios can trigger strong feelings, both positive and negative.

Given that link, it's no surprise that our emotional responses to money have a significant impact on our behaviors, whether we realize it or not. Experts have been studying this phenomenon through behavioral finance.

"Make behavioral finance an integral part of your investment journey, and you'll find that it offers not just the promise of financial growth but emotional enrichment as well," says Khwan Hathai, a certified financial planner (CFP) and certified financial therapist at Epiphany Financial Therapy in Denver.

WHAT IS BEHAVIORAL FINANCE?

Behavioral finance studies the intersection of psychology and finance to help explain why people make the financial decisions they do.

According to Rick Nott, a chartered financial analyst (CFA), CFP, and senior wealth advisor at LourdMurray in Los Angeles, traditional financial theories assume that everyone acts rationally and in their own best interests.

This premise, known as standard finance, operates under certain assumptions. For example, standard finance is built on the idea that people will always seek to manage the risk that's inherent in investing by reducing their risk as much as possible while maximizing their returns. It assumes they will act rationally based on data rather than on their emotions. It also assumes that financial markets are efficient.

But in the 1970s and 1980s, psychologists and economists joined forces and began to challenge that idea. Studies of the interplay between investors' feelings and subconscious and the financial market found that emotions played a larger role in people's financial decisions than was previously thought, and that the idea of the rational investor might be a fallacy.

Since then, behavioral finance has combined standard finance with psychology to study human behavior and how it affects our decision-making

process. These studies have confirmed that emotions often play a significant role in our financial decisions.

"Simply put, behavioral finance allows us to shift from asking what you should do with your money to why you are inclined to make certain financial decisions," Hathai says.

UNDERSTANDING BEHAVIORAL INVESTING

Behavioral investing, which is an aspect of behavioral finance, isn't just important to the psychologists and economists who study it. It has real-world impacts on individual investors. Understanding the emotions that might cause you to make certain decisions can help you rethink your investing choices to ensure they are in your best interests.

"When you comprehend your emotional triggers, you're better equipped to resist the siren call of impulsive decisions [and stay] anchored to a well-considered investment path. This kind of self-awareness is what [distinguishes] behavioral financial planning from traditional methods," says Hathai.

A perfect example of emotions influencing our actions is the concept

of panic selling—when people respond emotionally to stock market volatility and sell off their investments. Someone's instincts might tell them that selling is the right choice to avoid further losses.

But this behavior flies in the face of one of the core tenets of investing: Buy low, sell high. What's more, the record shows that the stock market has recovered from every crash in history. In fact, it's always gone on to reach new record highs. So as long as an investor has a well-diversified portfolio, there's no logical reason to believe their losses would be permanent. But when an emotional bias takes over, logic isn't in the driver's seat.

"I've spent 15 years working with individual investors, professionals, and investment groups," Nott says. "In those years, I've come to the conclusion that the behavioral aspect of investing will have a far greater impact on an investor's outcomes than the underlying investments that they choose."

BEHAVIORAL INVESTING IN THE STOCK MARKET

Understanding behavioral finance can also help us to understand why the stock market performs the way it does.

Standard finance and the efficient market hypothesis assume the stock market is efficient and accurately reflects all available information. In reality, movements in the stock market are entirely the result of human behavior. A company's stock price decline may have little to do with the company's performance but instead reflects investors' perceptions of the company's performance.

Consider the idea of panic selling, discussed above. A company's stock price—or the stock market as a whole—might experience a slight decline. But if investors start panic selling their investments, prices will

only decline more in a kind of self-fulfilling prophecy.

It's those investors who are able to see past their biases and make rational decisions who often come out ahead after major market events.

BIASES REVEALED BY BEHAVIORAL FINANCE

"There are two main categories of bias at the center of behavioral investing that negatively impact the way investors implement their strategies," Nott says.

The first category is cognitive bias, which is a systematic error in our thought processes that can affect our decisions and actions. If you think of your brain as a computer, cognitive bias is like an error in its programming.

"I like to think of these as the mind's version of an optical illusion," says Nott. "You can know it's an illusion and still see it as clear as day."

The second category is emotional bias, which is perhaps easier to understand. An emotional bias might cause us to act based on our feelings rather than the facts in front of us. For example, an emotional bias might cause us to panic sell our entire stock portfolio after a crash rather than wait for the market to recover.

"These are very hard to deal with because they can cause complete blindness in your decision-making," Nott says. "These are the types of things that might be obvious to everyone around you, but not you."

Here are a few common cognitive and emotional biases that can negatively impact someone's investing habits or success.

 Loss aversion: A financial loss feels more painful than a gain of the same amount. This could lead an investor to hold onto a low-performing stock for fear of locking in their losses or to refuse to accept any risk for a large potential return.

"The most important quality for an investor is temperament, not intellect."

—WARREN BUFFETT

Herding effect: People would rather follow the crowd than walk alone. This can lead to acting quickly driven by a fear of missing out, which could look like purchasing assets that aren't right for your portfolio.

 Anchoring: People anchor themselves to a particular belief and then use that as the basis for important decisions, even when the belief is factually incorrect or unrelated to the decision in question.

 Overconfidence: An investor may incorrectly gauge their ability to choose winning investments. Someone might make a rash decision rather than proceed with caution because they believe themselves to be an above-average investor.

 Status quo bias: Investors often default to what they already know. An investor might fail to change their investment strategy based on market changes, for example, or may be hesitant to invest when they've always held their savings in cash.

 Endowment effect: Investors tend to place a higher value on assets they already own than those they don't, even if those assets aren't necessarily better or more successful. As with the status quo bias, people stick with what they are comfortable with.

 Recency bias: People are more adept at recalling things that happened in the recent past. As a result, recent events can skew someone's investment strategy and cause them to ignore more relevant information that happens to be older.

OVERCOMING BIASES

Many of the cognitive and emotional biases defined above happen behind the scenes. In other words, they are influencing our financial decisions without us even realizing it. Given that reality, how can we overcome them to make more rational decisions?

A significant component of overcoming your biases is putting roadblocks in place to prevent them from taking over. One way to do this is by working with a financial professional, such as an advisor or CFP, or, depending on the depth of your biases, a mental health professional.

A professional can provide unbiased feedback about the your situation and discern your reasons for making your current decisions. Additionally, a financial professional can provide insight into historical examples that may ease your mind and help prevent you from acting impulsively.

Another way to stop your biases from taking over is to have a personal investment policy or an investment policy statement (IPS). An IPS is a document created with an advisor that lays out your investing objectives and strategies and outlines your risk tolerance and goals. Most important, it can outline how you'll proceed given certain market conditions.

Having an IPS in place can help you avoid making emotional decisions, because you drafted it with your advisor from a non-emotional place and might therefore rely on it in a moment of uncertainty rather than relying on your own instincts.

Finally, awareness is key. It's important to understand how your emotions affect your financial decision-making. A financial therapist can help you examine your behavior and determine what biases may be clouding your judgment and how you can overcome them.

"The next time you consider your investment choices, I invite you to take a moment to peer a little deeper," Hathai says. "Don't just look at the numbers; understand the emotional and psychological factors at play."

THE BOTTOM LINE

Behavioral finance isn't just a research area for financial and mental health professionals—it explores a phenomenon that affects everyone's financial behaviors and outcomes. The deep-rooted cognitive and emotional biases we all have can overwhelm our rational thinking and cause us to make decisions that aren't in our best interests. But with self-awareness, careful planning, and professional guidance, we can overcome those biases to reach our full financial potential. ➋

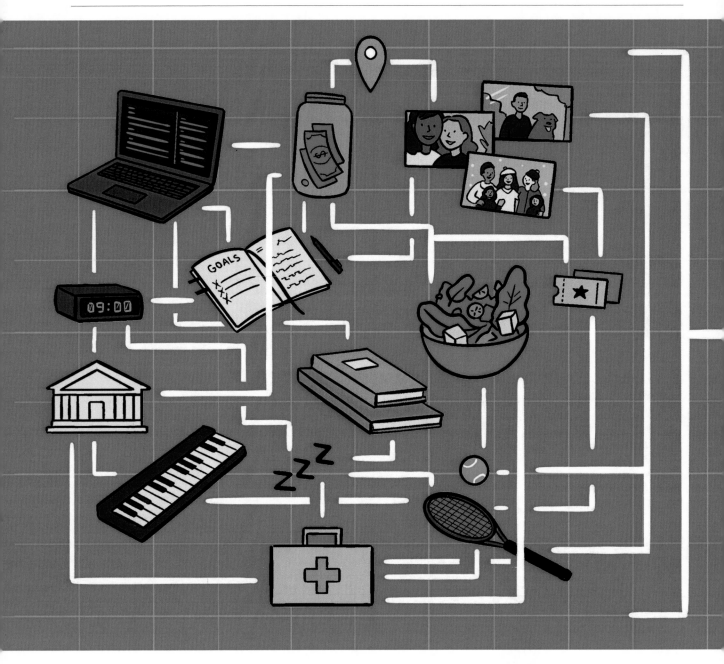

Why It Pays To Invest in Yourself

All the tangible and intangible rewards you'll get from focusing on No. 1

BY JESS FELDMAN

When you create an investment strategy, it's key to consider asset allocation—where to invest your time and money, and how much to spend on each category.

For each type of investment, there are general rules and guidelines investors often follow. When investing in retirement, for example, many experts recommend saving roughly 15% of your annual income. With a home, the expected down payment will

generally range from 5% to 20% of the price of the place you plan to buy.

But what about when it comes to investing in yourself? In other words, taking the time to focus on self-improvement, whether that means through seeking more education, practicing pottery as a hobby, or simply reserving 30 minutes a day for a walk out in nature.

How do we quantify the cost of something that, as Marie Kondo famously said, "brings us joy"?

According to Sarah O'Brien

Hammond, CEO of The NoW NYC, a community where women can learn and connect, the clarity and rules for this type of investment often come from a simple yet rare thing: taking the time to figure it out.

"I think that [investing in yourself] means making yourself a priority, which is not something that we—well, certainly as women—tend to do," O'Brien Hammond says. "And that means pausing. That means being able to rest. I think that is where everything begins."

IMPORTANT

Before launching a plan for your future, do an audit of where you are today—emotionally, financially, physically, and spiritually.

IT STARTS WITH VISUALIZING YOUR FUTURE

O'Brien Hammond worked as a corporate recruiter and then a managing consultant for over two decades, day in and day out, "subscribing to the societal definitions of success," she says.

Only when she took consistent time out of her day to meditate, do breathing exercises, or take a long walk did she realize that she had lost sight of the goals and passions that she really wanted to achieve in her life.

That was the opening she needed to reorient herself, which has paid off with the establishment of The NoW NYC and a successful consulting practice for women going through career transitions.

Today, O'Brien Hammond encourages her clients to adopt a similar practice to open up new avenues for work and fulfillment in their lives.

"I encourage my clients to dream … to sit in a space and daydream—look out the window and just allow yourself to be without an agenda, without a phone, without technology.… What can present itself?" she says.

You can apply a similar practice to your financial health and well-being. When Erika Wasserman, a certified financial therapist and founder of Miami-based Your Financial Therapist, meets with clients, she often engages them in what she calls vision work.

She might prompt a client by asking what they want to invest in financially. "If it's a home, I'll ask, what color is the home? Are the windows open? What noises are you hearing? Who's sitting at the kitchen table? What do you smell? And all of a sudden, you're investing not just in a house—you're investing in a home, in memories," Wasserman says. "That investment is very different than 'I have to put 20%

down on a home.'"

The value of these kinds of practices—imagining how you'll feel living in your own home, or seeing your children graduate from college, or switching to a new career—is that it creates a more visceral connection to that goal.

It's a way to make sure your financial goals really resonate with you and meet the needs of the person you want to be tomorrow, according to Elaine King, founder and CEO of the Miami-based Family and Money Matters Institute and an Investopedia 100 Top Financial Advisor.

"Money you can make, but timing you can't," King says. "I think investing in yourself means investing in your financial health, and that means not taking the brightest thing now but planting the seeds today. So that I not only have a tree, but from that tree I can have a forest."

WAYS TO INVEST IN YOURSELF

Every individual will have a different vision for their future, depending on their age, talents, financial situation, and overall interests.

If you're struggling to visualize how you might invest in yourself, here are some concrete ideas to get you started.

Create a Road Map

At the end of each year, King sits down and writes a letter to herself. The contents of this letter change annually, but they always include a list of what she truly wants to accomplish in the year ahead—and why—to be the best version of herself, as well as the steps she must take to reach her goals. (It's currently laminated and pinned above her desk, and she reviews it almost daily.)

Writing up the steps required to reach a goal is an essential part of investing in yourself. But according to

"You are the average of the five people you surround yourself with most, so I choose those people very wisely.… You must surround yourself with people who level you up if you, yourself, want to level up!"

—SARAH O'BRIEN HAMMOND
CEO of The NoW NYC

both King and O'Brien Hammond, outlining the why is the most important part. That's what will serve as your motivation, especially if there are unexpected roadblocks.

Another tip from O'Brien Hammond that she uses with clients: Before launching a plan for your future, do an audit of where you are today—emotionally, financially, physically, and spiritually.

"Where is your financial health? What resources can we identify for you [so you can] lower your stress and take actionable steps to achieving your goals?"

If you're not in good health in all of those areas, "it's like pushing a 10-ton boulder uphill," she says.

Learn Something New

While people often think learning stops if/when you graduate from higher education, in truth you are never too old to learn a new skill or hobby.

In doing so, you can learn to adapt better to change, increase your self-confidence, and improve your problem-solving abilities.

You might want to learn a new language, create a side business from your passion, as O'Brien Hammond did, or get certified in a skill that will enhance your career.

"Investing in myself was educating myself and being prepared for all the balls that were coming my way," King says of how she felt when she was first starting her financial planning business.

When King made the decision to become a business owner, she took applicable courses, increased her certifications, and consumed podcasts, articles, and specific information on the topic of financial planning daily.

"I thought, I don't need one certification, I need tons of certifications. I need to be not just prepared, but more than prepared."

For O'Brien Hammond, the first financial-specific investment she made when deciding to leave her 9-to-5 job was hiring a coach to help her figure out what direction she wanted her life to take.

"She gave me the space and permission, along with the necessary guidance, to come to all the answers myself, [which is now what I do for others]," O'Brien Hammond says.

For King, O'Brien Hammond, and Wasserman, the education they took on led them to a stronger sense of self-worth and confidence.

Prioritize Your Support System

When Wasserman was first starting her practice, surrounding herself with more-established entrepreneurs who provided mentorship was key to her success.

Not only just learning from them but observing them in their positions—and creating the vision of herself in their shoes—inspired her to keep going.

"I invested in people, and in return, they invested in me," Wasserman says.

Research shows that social support—essentially having a strong network of family and friends you can turn to in times of need—is key to good psychological health.

In fact, the subset of informational support, which involves guidance, advice, information, and mentoring, can help individuals feel less anxious when problem-solving or making big life decisions.

"You are the average of the five people you surround yourself with most, so I choose those people very wisely: People I admire [and] people that are doing what I want to be doing, living the life I aspire to live. You must surround yourself with people who level you up if you, yourself, want to level up!" O'Brien Hammond points out.

Address a Scarcity Mindset

In Wasserman's sessions with clients, she often sees a scarcity mindset—a pervasive, stressful feeling of not having enough money, or sometimes time or connection—come into play.

To combat that and help her clients feel like they can spend money on things that are not just essentials, she created the idea of a sunshine fund. Similar to a rainy day or emergency fund for savings in case of emergencies, the sunshine fund is money you set aside simply for your enjoyment.

"You don't want money to control your decisions," says King. "You want your strategic plan, your vision, your passion, your purpose, to drive those decisions."

THE BOTTOM LINE

Financial legend Warren Buffett is known for famously saying, "The most important investment you can make is in yourself." In his eyes, taking the time to consistently do something that you're passionate about will pave the way to long-term success.

There are no taxes involved in reading two books a month, and there's little risk in joining that choir you've always dreamt about. When you maximize yourself in a way that makes good sense for you, the return is that you will become the most valuable asset out there.

"The return on my investment in myself is beyond anything I could have ever imagined," O'Brien Hammond says. "I was living in the passenger seat of my own life. I was subscribing to someone else's definition of success. I didn't know who I was or what fulfilled me in life.

"Now I am consciously living each day with great intention and truly creating the life of my dreams. It is within everyone's reach if they just invest in themselves." ❷

True or False: Busting Popular Rules and Advice

Experts examine seven popular pieces of investing advice

BY ERIN GOBLER

O ne of the most challenging aspects of starting to invest is making sense of the deluge of advice available at your fingertips. It sometimes seems that every investing book, website, or expert shares the one thing that will make or break your investment success.

But what if the advice is bad—or only true with some context, or in certain situations? Just because an adage is timeworn doesn't mean it's trustworthy or good advice that you should follow. To help you sort the proverbial wheat from the chaff of investing know-how, we spoke with financial experts to identify seven

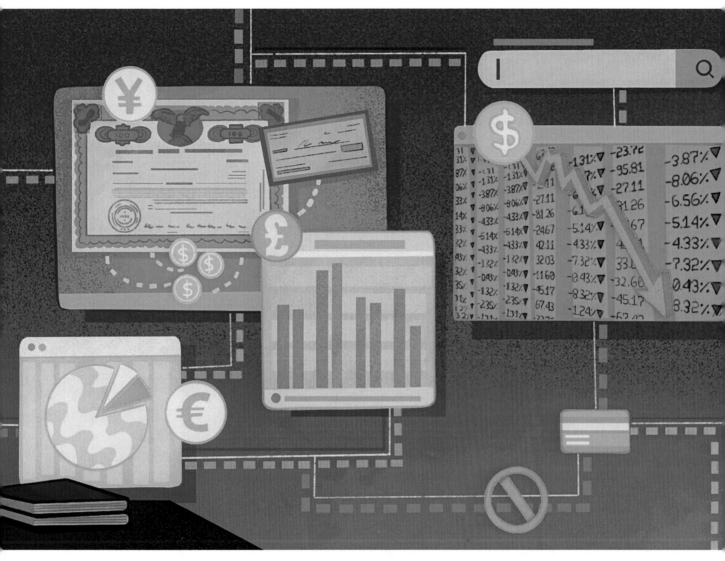

popular investing rules that may not be true (at least not for everyone).

"By challenging these investing rules, investors can develop a more nuanced and effective approach to their investment strategies, tailored to their individual goals, risk tolerance, and financial circumstances," says Nate Nead, investment banker and managing principal of Investnet, LLC, in Arkansas.

❌ DON'T INVEST UNTIL YOU'RE OUT OF DEBT

Many people believe they shouldn't dip into investing until they're no longer in the red. In fact, financial guru

Dave Ramsey teaches this in his famous Baby Steps program, encouraging people to wait until they're debt-free before starting to invest for retirement. But many financial experts disagree with this advice.

"Not all debt is created equal. In some cases, such as when you have high-interest credit card debt, it can make a lot of sense to pay that down before you invest," says Glenn Sanger-Hodgson, a certified student loan professional and financial planner at Shonan Gold Financial, LLC, in Florida. But as far as low-interest debt, such as your mortgage or an auto loan, he recommends investing while you continue to pay off those debts.

❌ BUY LOW, SELL HIGH

In a 1986 letter to Berkshire Hathaway Inc. shareholders, Warren Buffet famously said "…to be fearful when others are greedy and greedy when others are fearful." In other words, buy when asset prices are down and others are afraid to invest, and sell when prices are high and others are holding on for even higher returns.

This advice has become popular since then, but there's one problem with it: It's impossible to recognize a market high or low as it's happening. Even the best professional traders struggle to time the market properly, so recommending this strategy to a new investor is likely to set them up for failure.

"While this sounds simple and logical, in reality, predicting market highs and lows is incredibly challenging," says Andrew Latham, CFP, director of content at SuperMoney, a financial services website. "Instead of trying to time the market, individual investors should focus on a consistent, long-term investment strategy. Diversify your portfolio, keep learning, and don't make decisions based purely on emotion."

⊗ YOUR STOCK HOLDINGS SHOULD BE 100 MINUS YOUR AGE

When it comes to deciding on your portfolio's stock allocation, many people rely on a long-cited rule of thumb that says your stock holdings should equal a percentage of your portfolio that's equal to 100 minus your age.

So if you're 45, your stock holdings should make up about 55% of your portfolio, and the other 45% should be invested in lower-risk assets, such as bonds or money market funds.

But according to Kendall Meade, CFP, of SoFi, this advice too general and doesn't accommodate each person's unique situation and time horizon.

"How aggressively you should be invested depends on how comfortable you are with risk, as well as how long you have until you need the money," Meade says.

DIVERSIFY, DIVERSIFY, DIVERSIFY

In legendary investor Benjamin Graham's book *The Intelligent Investor,* he wrote, "Diversification is an established tenet of conservative investing." In the more than half-century since the book was written, it has remained one of the most widely touted investing rules.

But according to Reese Harper, CFP and CEO of the Elements Financial Monitoring System, this rule "has become a bit of a dogmatic term," and one that everyone should use differently to reach their own objectives.

Though diversification is one of the most important tenets of investing, the goal isn't necessarily to have the most diversified portfolio possible. Proper diversification will vary from person to person based on their risk tolerance, risk capacity, and financial goals. Additionally, diversification doesn't protect anyone from portfolio losses.

Rather than setting out to have the greatest number or variety of assets in your portfolio, focus on creating the asset allocation that best aligns with your financial situation and goals—even if that means being less diversified.

⊗ YOUR HOME IS YOUR BEST INVESTMENT

Real estate is one of the most popular investments in the United States. And while real estate investing can provide excellent income potential, many people also consider their home to be a form of investment. That could be a mistake. After all, while your home may be increasing in value over time like your stock investments, it may not result in a financial return in the end.

"What many fail to recognize are all the attendant costs of homeownership beyond the mortgage payment— property taxes, insurance, upkeep, etcetera," says Robert Johnson, a professor of finance at Creighton University's Heider College of Business. "Even before all those extra costs, home ownership has not proven to be a very sound investment over time beyond the important emotional value it provides for families."

From the period of March 1992

SCAN HERE

Check out Investopedia's Best Robo-Advisors list to find an automated investing tool that best supports your portfolio management needs.

through June 2023, housing prices experienced an average annual growth rate of 5.4%. During those same years, the stock market had average annual returns of 9.9%.

That difference doesn't even account for the costs of owning a home, such as maintenance, property taxes, homeowners insurance, and more. Meanwhile, the ownership costs of stock can be as low as $0 (though could be slightly higher if you own mutual funds or exchange-traded funds).

HIGH RISKS RESULT IN HIGH REWARDS

The famous investor and fund manager Peter Lynch has been quoted as saying, "You have to say to yourself, 'If I'm right, how much am I going to make? If I'm wrong, how much am I going to lose?' That's the right reward ratio."

In other words, an investor may be willing to accept higher potential losses in exchange for higher potential returns. However, the idea that high risk always results in high reward—or that all investors should accept a higher risk for higher rewards—should be taken with a big grain of salt.

"While this statement is generally true, it cannot be applied to all types of investors," says Raymond Quisumbing, a registered financial planner with BizReport. "Investors who are anxious about potential losses may not be well suited for high-risk investments." Emotional decision-making almost never ends well in the market. And accepting higher risk may not be appropriate for investors with a lower risk capacity, who can't afford to lose as much money.

Nor is the reward outcome a foregone conclusion. One dataset from the American Enterprise Institute shows that in the 10-year period from 2011 to 2020, the S&P 500 outperformed the average hedge fund, which typically invests in high-risk assets. And the potential losses for a high-risk investment can be much greater than they are for a low-risk one.

✕ RETIREMENT IS AN AGE, NOT A NUMBER

If we follow the cues of the Internal Revenue Service or the Social Security Administration, we might well believe that there's a certain age at which we should all retire. After all, the IRS only allows us to withdraw from our retirement accounts once we've reached a certain age, and the SSA has a "retirement age" in place at which people can start collecting benefits (typically 67).

According to Peter Salkins, CFP, a financial planner at Integrated Partners in Massachusetts, the concept of a specific retirement age dates back to a time when people often worked at the same company their entire working lives and retired with a pension.

Today, rather than thinking of retirement as an age, we should think of it as a number that can vary based on your goals. How much do you need to fund your desired retirement lifestyle, based on where you're at now?

For some, this approach may create additional financial stress. They may have always assumed they'd retire at 62, but their finances won't actually allow them to do that without some significant changes to their savings rate or investing strategy.

"For others who focus on creating and following a financial and investing plan, this can provide even more freedom," says Salkins. "You can build a plan that suits your life's goals, such as taking time off midcareer to travel the world, to truly retire early or later, start a new business, or focus your time volunteering."

| THE BOTTOM LINE |

With so much competing information available online—even from credentialed experts—it can be challenging to know which popular investing advice is worth following. Perhaps the most important takeaway from our interviews with financial experts is that few investing bromides apply universally to all investors or in all situations. Instead, each person must consider which investing rules align with their financial goals and should be followed—and which don't and may be set aside. ✷

3 More Fundamentals To Follow

These are the foundation of every good investment plan

BY ADAM HAYES

Investing can seem daunting, especially for those just starting out. With so many options and strategies to choose from, it's hard to know where to begin.

Here are three more guiding principles to help you find investing success no matter where you're starting out:

1 BE DISCIPLINED

With 24-7 financial news and constant stock ticker updates, it can be tempting to react to every market swing. But more often than not, knee-jerk responses do more harm than good. Investing is not just about numbers; it's about having a clear strategy, setting achievable goals, and maintaining them. Emotional reactions to market fluctuations can wreak havoc on your investments.

"Having a plan and sticking to it is crucial. Don't let fear or greed sway you from your investment strategy," says J. Sadler Hayes, president of Sadler Hayes Associates in New City, N.Y. Set your goals and asset allocation and rebalance periodically.

Avoid emotional decisions like selling all your stocks during a dip or chasing hot trends. Stay focused on the long term, keep perspective, and be patient.

2 INVEST REGULARLY

Investing isn't a sprint; it's more like a marathon. Consistency is key to making steady progress when you're investing over the long term. "It's far better to invest a little bit every month than to try timing the market with lump sums," says Martin A. Smith, an investment advisor and president of Wealthcare Financial Group in Peachtree, Ga. "If you try to time the market for when to jump in and out of it, you're likely to miss the best days over the long term."

Set up recurring automatic transfers of a fixed amount from your checking account to your investment account to take the emotion out of the process. Investing the same amount regularly means you buy more shares when prices are low and fewer when they're high—a strategy called dollar cost averaging.

Take full advantage of employer-sponsored retirement accounts with matching contributions, too. That's free money you don't want to miss out on. "Even if it's only 3% or 5% of your salary, make sure you're contributing at least enough to get the full match," advises Hayes.

3 ACCOUNT FOR INFLATION

While focusing on growth, don't overlook the subtle but corrosive effect of inflation. Over time, inflation erodes the purchasing power of your money—a dollar today won't buy nearly as much in 20 or 30 years (just as a dollar 30 years ago went a lot further than it does today). Your investments need to keep pace.

"Inflation really underscores the need to diversify across asset classes. For example, consider a reasonable allocation of commodities, like precious metals, timber, even agricultural products," says Andrew Wang, managing partner at Runnymede Capital Management in Morristown, N.J. "These tend to rise along with inflation even as other asset classes may struggle."

As you near retirement, consider treasury inflation-protected securities (TIPS). Their principal increases with inflation, providing a hedge. And periodically review your holdings to ensure you're poised to beat inflation.

THE BOTTOM LINE

By starting early, investing regularly, maintaining discipline, and accounting for inflation, you can set yourself up for investing success.

Follow these fundamentals, be patient and persistent, and your money can grow and provide you with a stable financial future. ⟳

Investopedia

The 10 Rules of Investing

EDITOR IN CHIEF Caleb Silver
SENIOR EDITORIAL DIRECTOR Anna Attkisson
EDITORIAL DIRECTOR, FINANCIAL PRODUCTS AND SERVICES Hilarey Gould
SENIOR EDITOR, TRADING & INVESTING Stella Osoba
SENIOR DIRECTOR, DATA JOURNALISM Amanda Morelli
SENIOR ART DIRECTOR Alice Morgan
SENIOR DATA REPORTER, DATA JOURNALISM Adrian Nesta
SENIOR EDITOR, SPECIAL PROJECTS Sienna Wrenn
EDITOR, SPECIAL PROJECTS Jess Feldman
ASSOCIATE EDITOR, TRADING AND INVESTING Katie Reilly
VICE PRESIDENT, BUSINESS PERFORMANCE AND STRATEGY Christine DiGangi
GENERAL MANAGER Dylan Zurawell

DOTDASH MEREDITH FINANCE SALES
PRESIDENT, ADVERTISING & PARTNERSHIPS Andrew Gorenstein
CHIEF REVENUE OFFICER Katherine Divney
SENIOR VICE PRESIDENT, CLIENT SERVICES Megan LaCava
VICE PRESIDENT, REVENUE STRATEGY Amber Macione
VICE PRESIDENT, SALES MARKETING Michael Capecci
VICE PRESIDENT, CONTENT STRATEGY Alec Morrison
VICE PRESIDENT, BRAND PARTNERSHIPS Bob Maund
VICE PRESIDENT, BRAND PARTNERSHIPS Emily Janocha
VICE PRESIDENT, PERFORMANCE MARKETING Jonathan Eng
DIRECTOR, ACCOUNT MANAGEMENT Matt Longo
DIRECTOR, CONTENT STRATEGY Irene Huhulea
DIRECTOR, CONTENT STRATEGY Al Smith
DIRECTOR, CLIENT SERVICES SOLUTIONS Holli Sorin
DIRECTOR, BRAND STRATEGY Meredith McCue
DIRECTOR, SALES MARKETING Alyssa Brady
DIRECTOR, SALES MARKETING Ariel Laub

DOTDASH MEREDITH PREMIUM PUBLISHING
EDITORIAL DIRECTOR Kostya Kennedy
CREATIVE DIRECTOR Gary Stewart
EDITORIAL OPERATIONS DIRECTOR Jamie Roth Major
MANAGER, EDITORIAL OPERATIONS Gina Scauzillo
ASSOCIATE MANAGER, EDITORIAL OPERATIONS Ariel Davis
PHOTO EDITOR Steph Durante
COPY CHIEF Tracy Guth Spangler
REPORTER Ryan Hatch
PRODUCTION DESIGNER Sandra Jurevics

VICE PRESIDENT & GENERAL MANAGER Jeremy Biloon
VICE PRESIDENT, GROUP EDITORIAL DIRECTOR Stephen Orr
SENIOR DIRECTOR, BRAND MARKETING Jean Kennedy
ASSOCIATE DIRECTOR, BRAND MARKETING Katherine Barnet
SENIOR MANAGER, BRAND MARKETING Geoffrey Wohlgamuth
BRAND MANAGER, BRAND MARKETING Mia Rinaldi

SPECIAL THANKS Gabby Amello, Brad Beatson

DOTDASH MEREDITH
CHIEF BUSINESS OFFICER & PRESIDENT, FINANCE, HEALTH & LIFESTYLE Alysia Borsa
DIRECTOR, BRAND MARKETING & COMMUNICATIONS Alexandra Kerr

Copyright © 2023 Dotdash Media Inc.
225 Liberty Street · New York, NY 10281
All rights reserved. No part of this book may be reproduced in any form or by any electronic or mechanical means, including information storage and retrieval systems, without permission in writing from the publisher, except by a reviewer, who may quote brief passages in a review.

For syndication or international licensing requests, email syndication.generic@dotdashmdp.com.
For reprint and reuse permission, email mmc.permissions@dotdashmdp.com.

PRINTED IN THE USA

This publication does not provide individual or customized legal, tax, accounting, or investment services. Since each individual's situation is unique, a qualified professional should be consulted before making financial decisions.

The Impact of Behavioral Investing on Your Portfolio p. 82

CREDITS

COVER Burazin/The Image Bank/Getty Images
P. 1 Mira Norian and Michela Buttignol
P. 2 Jordan Provost
PP. 4-7 Ellen Lindner
PP. 10-12 Alice Morgan
PP. 14-15 Julie Bang
PP. 16-31 Julie Bang
PP. 32-34 Tara Anand
PP. 38-39 Julie Bang
PP. 40-45 Jake Shi
PP. 46-51 Candra Huff
PP. 52-57 Dennis Madamba
PP. 58-63 Paige McLaughlin
PP. 64-67 Michela Buttignol
PP. 68-69 Michela Buttignol
PP. 70-71 Paige McLaughlin
PP. 72-73 Mira Norian
PP. 74-75 Mira Norian
PP. 76-77 Julie Bang
PP. 78-81 Michela Buttignol
PP. 82-85 Joules Garcia
PP. 86-89 Hilary Allison
PP. 90-93 Zoe Hansen
P. 95 Joules Garcia

SCAN HERE

Learn more about Investopedia's mission, policies, history, and staff.

How the Fed Funds Rate Impacts the Market

BY ANNA ATTKISSON

The Federal Open Market Committee (FOMC) is the monetary policymaking body of the Federal Reserve that holds eight meetings a year, and may hold other meetings as necessary. The 12 members of the FOMC review economic and financial conditions to determine the right next steps for the U.S. economy.

In March 2022, the committee began what would become an ongoing battle to reduce inflation to a 2% target range by raising the Federal Funds Rate regularly.

The Fed Funds Rate is the target interest rate range at which commercial banks borrow and lend excess reserves to each other overnight. This, in turn, impacts interest rates across the economy for products such as mortgages and credit cards.

This rate-hiking campaign has been the most aggressive since the 1980s, and impacts the value of assets and the U.S. dollar, thus potentially impacting the stock market—but not always. ↻

Interest Rate Changes vs. the S&P 500 Index

The Fed Funds Rate may help the balance the economy, but it's not indicative of what the stock market does. Per Rule No. 2, the economy isn't the market—and vice versa.

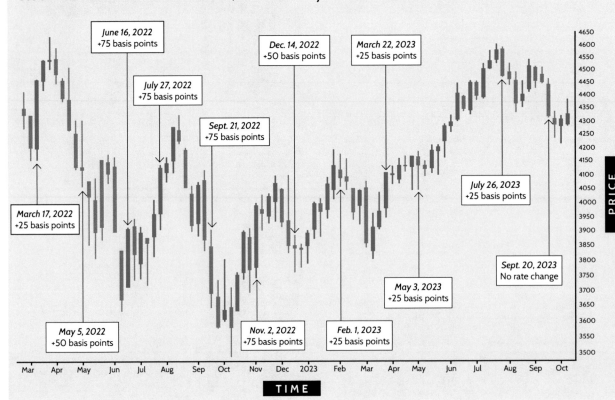

Your Opinion Matters To Us!

Tell us what you think of this special issue by taking the survey at investopedia.com/readersurvey

Enter to Win a $100 Gift Card*

⊘ Investopedia

* NO PURCHASE OR SURVEY PARTICIPATION IS NECESSARY TO ENTER OR WIN. Subject to Official Rules at http://www.investopedia. com/sweepstakes. The 2023-2024 Investopedia Reader Survey Sweepstakes begins at 12:00 AM ET on 12/15/23 and ends at 11:59 PM ET on 4/7/24. Open to legal residents of the 50 United States and the District of Columbia, 21 years or older. Sweepstakes is offered by Dotdash Media Inc. and may be promoted by any of its publications in various creative executions online and in print at any time during the sweepstakes. Limit one (1) entry per person and per email address, per survey invitation. Void where prohibited. Sponsor: Dotdash Media Inc.

JAN 1 7 2024

Made in United States
North Haven, CT
05 January 2024

47093681R00055